To Bruce Bloom —
A great writer
and marketing
man!

Best wishes,

11-15-08

Bly on Direct Marketing

MeritDirect Press

MeritDirect Press publishes books that assist multi-channel direct marketers to become more successful and profitable. Established by the partners of MeritDirect, a leading business-to-business list brokerage and management firm, the mission of MeritDirect Press is to bring knowledge and wisdom of multi-channel direct marketing to clients and the direct marketing community.

MeritDirect Press
333 Westchester Avenue
White Plains, New York 10604
Telephone: (914) 368-1000
www.meritdirect.com

Editorial Offices
280 South 79th Street Suite 1401
West Des Moines, Iowa 50266
Telephone: (515) 537-2307

Manuscripts for books on multi-channel direct marketing are welcomed and may be sent to the editorial offices by email.

To order books direct from the publisher:
www.MeritDirect.com or (866) 405-1300

Bly on
Direct Marketing

258 Ways to Double Your Response—
Based on a Quarter Century of Proven Results

by
Robert W. Bly

MERITDIRECT PRESS
WHITE PLAINS, NEW YORK

Acknowledgements

Thanks to Ralph Drybrough, Don Libey, and the team at MeritDirect Press for agreeing to bring this book to a new audience. Additional thanks to the experts who share their advice in these pages, especially those who allowed me to interview them so I could pass their knowledge on to you. Finally, thanks to the editors of *DM News, Subscription Marketing, Early to Rise, Internet Media Review, Writer's Digest* and other publications where most of these chapters originally appeared in slightly different form.

ISBN 0-9765172-1-3 (acid-free paper)

Published in the United States of America by MeritDirect Press

MeritDirect Press
333 Westchester Avenue
White Plains, New York 10604
(914) 368-1000

Book Sales and Customer Service
MeritDirect Press
Toll-free: (866) 405-1300

Printed on acid-free paper.
Manufactured in the United States of America.
First Edition

Cover, typography and layout design by Angela Schmitt, Accent Design, Des Moines, Iowa.

This book is for Ralph Drybrough, Don Libey,
Clayton Makepeace, and Paul Goldberg.

Contents

Contents

Contents

Introduction

Many direct marketers spend a large part of their careers searching in vain for the 'silver bullet' . . . the magic direct response principles, ideas, or tactics that work in every situation and can ensure that each promotion is a resounding winner.

Of course, no such silver bullet exists. Or if one does exist, I certainly don't have it, nor does anyone else I know. If I did have it, well . . . Bill Gates would be my houseboy. I would be rich beyond the dreams of avarice—and most likely, the richest man on the planet.

Why has the silver bullet for winning direct response never been found? Because every product, every market and every promotion is different. What works for one market fails in another. What works for one product flops for a second, even though the two products seem very much alike. A package that pulls like gangbusters on one list fails to break even on another. A promotional concept that worked great last year fizzles this year.

Yet, there is a ray of hope. Even though direct marketing success is largely a moving target, some principles, ideas, and tactics do work in the majority of cases. We know, for example, that direct mail pulls better when you use the word 'free' . . . and that email marketing generates more response when it is based on current events or news.

In this book, you get dozens of suggestions, strategies, recommendations, and rules of thumb with the potential to double or triple your response rates—giving you more leads and sales, and increasing your marketing return on investment many times over.

These methods are based on accumulated knowledge acquired during my quarter of a century of writing direct mail, space ads, landing pages, email marketing campaigns, and other promotions for more than one-hundred clients ranging from small businesses to middle market companies to Fortune 500 corporations.

This is the third volume of my collected articles. The first, *Quick Tips for Better Business-to-Business Marketing Communications*, was published by the Business Marketing Association in 1997, and is still available from them today (www.marketing.org). The second, *Bob Bly's Guide to Freelance Writing Success* (Filbert), collects my articles for freelance writers.

All of the articles in this book were written after the BMA book was published. Therefore, they embrace Internet marketing and fully reflect the changes the Internet has made to marketing and commerce.

Also, while this book reflects my opinions, methods, and beliefs based on my quarter century of direct marketing experience, they do not necessarily reflect the opinions of MeritDirect, MeritDirect Press, or its staff.

I do have one favor to ask. If you have a direct response technique I have not covered, please send it to me so I can share it with readers of the next edition of this book. You will receive full credit, of course. To contact me:

Bob Bly
Copywriter
22. E. Quackenbush Avenue
Dumont, NJ 07628

Phone (201) 385-1220
Fax (201) 385-1138
email: rwbly@bly.com
web: www.bly.com

Bly on Direct Marketing

Part I Marketing

CHAPTER 1

Four Stages of Marketing Competence

During my quarter of a century as a copywriter, I have observed that business owners and managers fall into one of four categories as far as their competence and skill in marketing is concerned. By recognizing which category you are in and taking the action steps recommended below, you can move up to the next level and significantly increase the ROI from your marketing dollars.

A realistic assessment of your level of marketing competency can also guide you as to when to listen to a consultant or advisor and when to ignore his or her advice because your instincts tell you it is wrong.

UNCONSCIOUS INCOMPETENCE

The lowest level of marketing competence is *unconscious incompetence*. You don't know what you are doing, and worse, you don't know that you don't know. You may even think you are a pretty sharp marketer, even though to others, that is clearly not the case. Egotistical small business owners who appear in their own TV commercials and junior employees at 'creative' Madison Avenue ad agencies can fall into this category.

Do you think you are an okay marketer, and blame the lack of results generated by your marketing always on external factors, such as bad timing, bad lists, or bad luck? You are probably in the unconscious incompetence stage. Recognize that you don't know what you're doing and it is hurting your business. Get help. Hire a marketing manager who knows more than you do. Or take a marketing course or workshop.

CONSCIOUS INCOMPETENCE

The next stage up the ladder is *conscious incompetence*. You've recognized that the reason your marketing isn't working is that you don't know what you're doing. Again, take the steps recommended above. When I was at this stage as an advertising manager recently graduated from college and with only a year of work experience under my belt (instead of the considerable paunch that resides there now), I hired an experienced ad agency and leaned on them for guidance. This strategy worked well for me and for my employer. The company got better advertising than I could have produced on my own. And working with the agency accelerated my own marketing education, making me a more valuable employee.

Conscious incompetence is better than unconscious incompetence because people in the former stage are amenable to guidance, while those in the latter stage are not. My friend Jim Alexander, founder of business-to-business ad agency Alexander Marketing in Grand Rapids, Michigan, once told me: "I can handle a client who is ignorant *or* arrogant, but not one who is both." The unconscious incompetent is often both.

CONSCIOUS COMPETENCE

Moving higher up the ladder of marketing competence, you reach the stage of *conscious competence*. You've read the books, taken the courses, and understand what works. But your experience at putting it into practice is limited. That means whenever you want to create a promotion, you have to slow down and think about what you are doing. It doesn't come naturally.

In this stage, you should keep checklists, formulas, and swipe files (examples of successful promotions you admire) close at hand. Model your own efforts after the winners of others. Don't try to reinvent the wheel. Observe what works and adapt it to your own product and market. Do this enough times, and you will slowly begin to become a true master of marketing, reaching the next and highest level of marketing competence.

UNCONSCIOUS COMPETENCE

At the stage of *unconscious competence*, coming up with great offers, promotional ideas, headlines, and copy are second nature to you. You do it naturally, without having to consult your checklists or reference files. The quality of your work is better, and it comes faster and easier.

However, you should still keep an extensive swipe file of promotions. Borrowing ideas and inspiration from direct mail packages that are working is a time-honored tradition in our industry, as long as it does not step over into plagiarism or copyright infringement.

My colleague Michael Masterson says it takes approximately 1,000 hours of practice to become really competent at copywriting, marketing, playing the flute, or anything else. If you have expert guidance, you may be able to cut that to 500 hours. But ultimately, you learn by doing—and doing a lot. If you are at this stage, keep doing more and more marketing. When you put in 5,000 hours, you will become great, not just good, and your results will be even better.

Action steps: Rank yourself using the four levels of marketing competence as described; follow the recommendations for improving and moving to the next higher stage.

CHAPTER 2

When Does Advertising Become Deceptive?

Was Blockbuster lying to us? Some people think so. Blockbuster's commercials promised, "The end of late fees." But of course, that was impossible: if there is no penalty for returning a movie late, you could keep it forever. The way it really worked was this: there was no late fee when you kept a movie a few extra days. But if you didn't return the movie within seven days, you were forced to buy it at the retail price. Even then, you could still return the movie you 'purchased' within thirty days for "a restocking fee plus applicable taxes." After that, you bought the movie permanently and it was yours.

TRUTH OR DECEPTION?

Did that make "the end of late fees" a truthful or deceptive claim? In my opinion, the latter—they were lying to consumers, pure and simple. "The end of late fees" was trumpeted in Blockbuster's prime time TV spots. But the 'fine print' of the deal was printed in a little booklet you got—at my local Blockbuster anyway—only if you asked for it.

"It is deceptive at best," wrote marketing consultant Jim Logan. "I have rented my last DVD/video from Blockbuster. What Blockbuster is doing is ruining their relationship with their customers. They have big banners in front of their stores that read 'The

End of Late Fees.' To have any type of late fee now just establishes them as a company that doesn't take their customers seriously. Any company that engages in deceptive advertising cannot be trusted. Common sense would suggest this practice will alienate a good number of their customers and have a negative effect on their revenue."

PERCEPTIONS IN DIRECT MARKETING LANGUAGE

So, what does all this have to do with direct marketing? Simply that it speaks to the issue of how far we can go in creating perceptions about our products and services versus describing them flat-out in literal, accurate, to-the-letter language.

A VP at a major direct marketing publisher recently described direct marketing promotions as "controlled hyperbole." But the separation between hyperbole and fact is often gray, not black and white. For instance, it's true that Blockbuster technically did away with the 'late fees' as they once had them. But one can argue that the difference between the old late policy and the ill-fated revised late policy was merely semantics.

How about when you tell the consumer in your mailing that he may try your product free for thirty days? Actually, in a hard offer mailing, it isn't free because they have to send money. The average consumer doesn't think of something as free when she has to mail you a check to get it.

What about soft offers? Many subscription promotions with a thirty-day money-back guarantee promote the first issue, sent within thirty days, as a 'free issue.' In reality, that issue is free only if you do *not* become a subscriber. If you do subscribe, then you are paying for that issue. For a monthly publication, that first issue is one of a total of twelve you will get as part of your one-year subscription. So, for those who pay and do not request a refund, there *is* no free issue. In that case, 'free issue' is not wholly accurate. More correctly, we should say 'risk-free issue' or 'no-risk issue.' To make it a true *free* issue, you would have to give them the first issue plus twelve more issues (if they subscribe)—a total of thirteen issues for the price of twelve.

PERCEPTIONS IN DIRECT MARKETING FORMATS

Even formats can be deceptive. What about those mailings that *appear* to be a check showing through the envelope window? Or those mailings that look like articles torn out of a magazine or newspaper with a yellow post-it note attached that says, "Try this. –J.," and you have no idea who J. is? Or ads in the newspaper—or those sections in magazines—that look like articles, but are really paid ads? Or those postcards and vouchers that look like they came from an official government agency?

ETHICAL BENCHMARKS

Of course, we know that consumers are wary and skeptical of advertising. And we know that making our promotions look informational or official can often lift response. But how do you know when you've gone too far? Three important indicators to pay attention to: (a) your own sense of ethics, (b) the law, and (c) consumer reaction.

The bottom line is this: if your gut tells you that your promotion is deceptive, it probably is. And you should probably fix it.

CHAPTER 3

How to Charge and Get a Premium Price for Your Product

"I want to charge $399 for my audio cassette album," a small publisher told me.

"But Nightingale-Conant also sells several audio albums on the same topic for $79," I pointed out. "What makes yours worth five times more than theirs?"

The answer most people would give is "because mine is better." Well, maybe it is. But 'better' is a difficult proposition to sell through a direct mail package.

So how can you charge a premium price to buyers to whom the greater quality of your product is not immediately obvious? Here are a few ways to ask for and get the price you want:

VERTICAL NICHE

The more vertical your product, the higher the price you can charge. Your total audience will be smaller, but their need for a specific solution to their problem will help them rationalize paying your premium price. A "Selling Techniques" album priced at $399 is difficult to promote, but you might be able to get $399 for "Selling Techniques for the Automotive Aftermarket."

SUPPLY AND DEMAND

It's always easier—especially when selling your services—to hold out for more money when the demand for your service outweighs the supply. If you market to the point where you are generating more potential business opportunities than you can handle, you can raise your fees, because you can afford to have some of these potential buyers who balk at the higher fees walk away. For service providers, the surest route to financial security is a full pipeline of leads.

ADD VALUE

Add value to your product or service until the buyer perceives that the price you are asking, however high, is a drop in the bucket compared to the value he is receiving.

One way to add value is to offer a premium that is inexpensive for you to source but has a high perceived value. Example: Ron Popeil gives away a set of steak knives free when you buy his cooker on TV.

Mike Bell at Phillips Publishing suggests you give premiums whose total value is greater than the cost of the product. That way, even if the buyer doesn't love your product, he may keep it just to own the free gifts he received along with it.

BECOME A GURU

Whether it's Tom Peters, Alan Dershowitz, or Dr. Ruth, people can't get enough of gurus. Make an effort to build your reputation and establish yourself as a guru—a leading expert—in your field. When you are a guru, people will pay a premium price for your seminars, speeches, videos, audios, books, newsletters, software, and products.

DEMONSTRATE RETURN ON INVESTMENT (ROI)

Buyers are less reluctant to pay a high price when you can show that they will get a rapid—and significant—return on their investment.

For instance, a direct mail package selling a $149 newsletter on employee hiring says, "Hiring the wrong person costs you three times their annual salary." The reader figures that if his average employee makes $50,000, and the newsletter can prevent even one hiring mistake, his return on investment for a subscription is 3 X $50,000 = $150,000 divided by $149, or better than 1,000 to 1—which makes the $149 asking price an easy sell.

UNIQUE SYSTEM

Despite the glut of free stock tips and financial information available on the Internet, a direct mail package from Agora Publishing successfully sold a $59 a year newsletter with this headline, "Unlock Wall Street's Hidden Logic."

Why did it work? It offered the reader something he felt he couldn't get from all the free websites and email newsletters he was offered: the secret to how the stock market really works—Wall Street's hidden logic. If the customer perceives he cannot get what you offer elsewhere, he will pay a premium price for it, provided the product offers benefits he desires.

GUARANTEE

A guarantee overcomes buyer resistance, including price resistance. When your product is backed by a thirty-day money-back guarantee, you can offer a 'no-risk trial' or 'risk-free thirty-day subscription' rather than just say "buy my product." In essence, you are not asking the reader to buy anything; merely to *try* it—to accept your offer of examining it for a month in their home or office, with no risk or obligation of any kind.

To dramatize the low risk of a money-back offer, recommend to the reader that he postdates his check one month from today—then tell him you will hold his check for a full thirty days. If he asks for a refund, promise to return his uncashed check—or one of equal value—to him.

CHAPTER 4

Understand Your Customer's Core Buying Complex with the *BFD* Formula

How well do you really know your customers? Reading the list data cards is a good way to learn something about the folks you mail to, but it's not enough. Knowing that you are writing to farmers, information technology professionals or plumbers is just the start. You have to dig deeper.

UNDERSTAND MOTIVATIONS

To write powerful copy, you must go beyond the demographics to understand what motivates these people—who they are, what they want, how they feel and what their problems and concerns are that your product can help solve. One direct marketer told me, "We want to reach prospects on three levels: intellectual, emotional and personal."

INTELLECTUAL APPEAL

Intellectual is the first level and, though effective, is weaker than the other two. An intellectual appeal is based on logic, such as, "Buy the stocks we recommend in our investment newsletter and you will beat the market by fifty to one hundred percent."

EMOTIONAL APPEAL

More powerful is to reach the prospect on an emotional level. Emotions that can be tapped include fear, greed, love, vanity and, for fundraising, benevolence. Using our example of a stock market newsletter, the emotional appeal might be, "Our advice can help you cut your losses and make much more money so you become much wealthier than your friends and neighbors. You'll be able to pay cash for your next car—a Lexus, BMW or any luxury automobile you care to own—and you'll sleep better at night."

PERSONAL APPEAL

The most powerful way you can reach people is on a personal level. Again, from the stock market newsletter: "Did you lose a small fortune in the April 2000 tech stock meltdown? So much that it put your dreams of retirement or financial independence on hold? Now you can gain back everything you lost, rebuild your net worth and make your dream of early retirement or financial independence come true—a lot sooner than you think."

THE BUYER'S CORE COMPLEX

To reach prospects on all three levels—intellectual, emotional, and personal—you must understand what copywriter Michael Masterson calls the buyer's *Core Complex*. These are emotions, attitudes and aspirations that drive them, as represented by the formula *BFD*: beliefs, feelings and desires.

Beliefs. What does your audience believe? What is their attitude toward your product and the problems or issues it addresses?

Feelings. How do they feel? Are they confident and brash? Nervous and fearful? What do they feel about the issues in their lives, businesses or industries?

Desires. What do they want? What are their goals? What change do they want in their lives that your product can help them achieve?

For instance, we did this exercise using IT people as the prospect group for a company that gives seminars in communication and interpersonal skills for IT professionals. Here's what we came up with in a group meeting:

Beliefs. IT people think they are smarter than other people are, technology is the most important thing in the world, users are stupid and management doesn't appreciate them enough.

Feelings. IT people often have an adversarial relationship with management and users, both of whom they service. They feel others dislike them, look down upon them and do not understand what they do.

Desires. IT people want to be appreciated and recognized. They also prefer to deal with computers and avoid people whenever possible. And they want bigger budgets.

Based on this analysis, particularly the feelings, the company created a direct mail letter, its most successful ever, to promote a seminar titled, "Interpersonal Skills for the IT Professional." The headline: "Important news for any IT professional who has ever felt like telling an end user, 'Go to hell.'"

Before writing copy, write out in narrative form the *BFD* of your target market. Share this with your team and reach an agreement on it. Then write copy based on the agreed *BFD*.

START WITH PROSPECTS, NOT PRODUCTS

Copywriter Don Hauptman advises, "Start with the prospect, not the product." With *BFD*, you quickly gain a deeper understanding of your prospects before you try to sell them something. Stronger marketing campaigns usually follow.

Occasionally, insights into the prospect's desires and concerns can be gleaned through formal market research. For instance, a copywriter working on a cooking oil account was reading a focus group transcript and came across this comment from a user: "I fried chicken in the oil and then poured the oil back into a measuring cup. All the oil was there except one tablespoon." This comment, buried in the appendix of a focus group report, became the basis of a successful TV campaign dramatizing that most of the oil had returned and therefore the chicken was not greasy when cooked in it.

Veteran ad man Joe Sacco once had an assignment to write a campaign for a new needle used by diabetics to inject insulin. What was the key selling point?

The diabetics Sacco talked with praised the needle because it was sharp. A non-user probably would view being sharp as a negative. But if you have given yourself or anyone else an injection, you know that sharper needles go in smoother, with no pain. Sacco wrote a successful ad campaign based on the claim that these needles were sharp, thus enabling easier, pain-free insulin injections.

Part II

Direct Marketing

CHAPTER 5

Three Components of a Winning Unique Selling Proposition

In 1961, Rosser Reeves published his classic book, *Reality in Advertising,* in which he introduced the notion of the *Unique Selling Proposition,* or USP. Today the book is out of print and difficult to get. As a result, most practicing direct marketers don't know the original definition of a USP. Their lack of knowledge often produces USPs that are weak and ineffective. According to Reeves, there are three requirements for a USP (and I am quoting, in the italics, from *Reality in Advertising* directly):

1. *Each advertisement must make a proposition to the consumer. Each must say, "Buy this product, and you will get this specific benefit."* Your headline must contain a benefit—a promise to the reader.

2. *The proposition must be one that the competition either cannot, or does not, offer.* Here's where the 'unique' in Unique Selling Proposition comes in. It is not enough merely to offer a benefit. You must also *differentiate* your product.

3. *The proposition must be so strong that it can move the mass millions, i.e., pull over new customers to your product.* The differentiation cannot be trivial. It must be a difference that is very important to the reader.

Why do so many advertisements fail? One reason is that the marketer has not formulated a strong USP for his product and built his advertising upon it. Formulating a USP isn't difficult, but it does take some thinking; and many people don't like to think. But, when you start creating direct mail and advertising without first thinking about what your USP is, your marketing is weak because there is nothing in it to compel the reader to respond. It looks and sounds like everyone else, and what it says isn't important to the reader.

In general advertising for packaged goods, marketers achieve differentiation by building a strong brand at a cost of millions or even billions of dollars. Coca-Cola has an advantage because of its brand. If you want a cola, you can get it from a dozen soda makers. But if you want a Coke, you can only get it from Coca-Cola. Intel has achieved a similar brand dominance, at an extraordinary cost, with its Pentium line of semiconductors.

Most direct marketers are too small and have too strong a need to generate an immediate positive ROI from their marketing to engage in this kind of expensive brand building. So we use other means to achieve the differentiation in our USP. One popular method is to differentiate your product or service from the competition based on a feature that your product or service has and they don't. The common error here is building the USP around a feature that, while different, is unimportant to the prospect, and therefore unlikely to move him to try your product or service. For example, in the pump industry, it is common for pump manufacturers to attempt to win customers by advertising a unique design feature. Unfortunately, these design twists often result in no real performance improvement; no real advantage that the customer can perceive.

Realizing that they could not differentiate based on a concrete design principle, Blackmer pump took a different tack: to create a USP based upon *application* of the product. Their trade ads showed a Yellow Pages ripped out of an industrial buying guide, full of listings for pump manufacturers, including Blackmer. Their company name was circled in pen. The headline of the ad read, "There are only certain times you should call Blackmer for a pump. Know when?" Body copy explained (and I am paraphrasing here), "In many applications, Blackmer pumps perform no better or worse than any other pumps, and so we are not a particularly advantageous choice. But," the ad went on, "for certain applications (viscous fluids, fluids containing abrasives, slurries, and a few other situations) Blackmer is proven to outperform all other pumps, and is the logical brand of choice." Blackmer closed the ad by offering a free technical manual proving the claim. My old friend, Jim Alexander, of Alexander Marketing in Grand Rapids, Michigan, created this campaign and tells me it worked extremely well.

The easiest situation in which to create a strong USP is when your product has a unique feature—one that competitors lack—that delivers a strong benefit. This must be an advantage the customer really cares about, not one that, though a difference, is trivial.

But what if such a proprietary advantage does not exist? What if your product is basically the same as the competition, with no special features? Reeves has the answer here, too. He said the uniqueness can either stem from a strong brand (already discussed as an option ninety-five percent of marketers can't use) or from "a claim not otherwise made in that particular form of advertising"—that is, other products may have this feature too, but advertisers haven't told consumers about it.

An example from packaged goods advertising: "M&Ms melt in your mouth, not in your hand." Once M&M established this claim as their USP, what could the competition do? Run an ad that said, "We *also* melt in your mouth, not in your hand!?"

In his book, *Scientific Advertising*, Claude Hopkins gives an example of a USP that has become a classic story. The short version: an ad man walking through his beer client's brewery was fascinated by a machine that blasted steam into beer bottles to sanitize them. "Don't use that in advertising," the brewer told the ad man. "It is nothing unique; every brewer does the same."

"Maybe," the ad man replied, "but I had never heard of it before, and neither has any of the beer-drinking public." He then created a successful ad campaign for a beer advertised as, "so pure the bottles are washed in live steam."

One more point: as direct marketers, we—unlike most general advertisers today—are compelled to create advertising that generates net revenues in excess of its cost. Reeves believed all advertising had to do this. He defined advertising as, "the art of getting a USP into the heads of the most people at the lowest possible cost." If I were to modify his definition, I would change it to, "getting a USP into the heads of the people *most likely to buy the product*, at the lowest possible advertising cost." But who am I to quibble with the master?

CHAPTER 6

Increase Customer Satisfaction of Direct Response Buyers

Are there certain industries whose business model is dependent on *not* helping customers—businesses designed to actually be more profitable when *not* giving customers the best advice, products, and service? Here are some that have been suggested to me by various people:

1. *Insurance.* My late father, an insurance agent for five decades, once said, "Insurance companies want to write fire insurance policies for pig iron at the bottom of the ocean." They want to collect fat premiums for policies they will never have to pay off, and often make it difficult for policyholders to collect on legitimate claims.

2. *HMOs and others in 'managed care.'* See 1 above.

3. *The pharmaceutical industry.* It is much more profitable to create an expensive drug you have to take for the rest of your life rather than cure the illness or eliminate the condition (e.g., high blood pressure). As comic Chris Rock points out in one of his comedy routines, "There's no money in curing; the money's in the medicine."

4. *Psychotherapists.* If the psychotherapist quickly cures every patient in a few weeks, the lifetime value of each client diminishes drastically. There's a financial incentive to drag treatment out over the course of many years.

5. *Chiropractors.* See 4 above.

6. *Stock brokers.* Wall Street is rigged against the individual investor. Brokers are told to push shares their firms underwrite, not those stocks that are the best investment.

7. *Business consultants.* They ask to borrow your watch and then charge you for telling you what time it is. The consultant or coach gets paid whether you get results or not. The consultant who teaches the client to do it on their own often finds himself out of a job.

8. *Advertising agencies* (specifically: general, not direct response). They have a financial incentive to sell you ad campaigns that are: (a) the most elaborate and expensive (increases billings); and (b) win creative awards (which helps win them new business). We see the latter even in direct response ad agencies: the campaigns that win awards are much more often splashy, creative, colorful, and dimensional mailings; rarely is the award-winning package a plain typed sales letter.

9. *Higher education.* There is a growing trend of encouraging students to take an extra year to earn a bachelors degree, which sets the student back in his career and financial progress while allowing the school to collect an extra year's tuition.

10. *Lawyers.* "In most lawyers, there is a sense that if the problem is solved, the billable hours will end," says attorney Douglas Sorocco.

I don't mean to imply that everyone, or even the majority, of practitioners in these fields are out to cheat customers. I am simply observing that there is an incentive inherent in each business model *not* to always do what is best for the customer (which a smart practitioner knows is canceled out by the business benefits of delivering superior customer satisfaction). Would you dispute any of the above? Or do you agree wholeheartedly? Any other industries you would add to the list?

People outside our industry often accuse direct marketing of being sleazy or deceptive, but the fact is, the direct marketing business model is inherently slanted almost totally in the customer's favor. The factor dictating that we must treat our customers like gold and deliver more value for their money is the return on investment of direct marketing: namely, that the mathematics of direct marketing make it virtually impossible to be profitable on the 'front-end,' or initial sale, and almost every profitable direct marketing company makes its money on the back-end sales. To do that, you must consistently deliver superior customer satisfaction to generate the repeat orders that maximize customer lifetime value. So how do you deliver superior customer satisfaction to your direct marketing customers? Here are five timeless suggestions:

1. Don't just give the customer their money's worth. Give them more for their money than they have any right to expect.

2. Honor your guarantee without quibble or hassle. Give prompt, full refunds politely and without any hedging or attempt to weasel out of your guarantee. When in doubt, err on the site of being too generous rather than too strict.

3. Make it easy for the customer to communicate with you in the way they prefer. For instance, if you are an online business, don't—like Amazon—make it difficult for customers to talk to a live customer service person on the phone, if that is what they prefer. And provide a toll-free number for doing so.

4. Offer loyalty programs, bonus points, volume discounts, and free gifts to your best customers: the more customers spend with you, the more preferential treatment they should get.

5. Resolve complaints and problems quickly, giving customers extraordinary resolution. For instance, the CEO of a major catalog marketer not only refunds the customer's money or offers replacement merchandise, but also writes a personal letter to the customer and sends a free gift by way of apology.

Anything else you'd add to this list?

CHAPTER 7

Why Branding and Direct
Marketing *Don't* Mix

Should direct marketers worry about branding? "Yes," says Steve Cuno, chairman of RESPONSE Prospecting and Loyalty Strategies, in an article in *Deliver* (July 2005), a magazine published by the U.S. Postal Service. "As a direct marketer, you're hired to pull a profitable, measurable response, not to build the brand," says Steve. Well, at least Steve's got that part right. But then he goes on, "If you don't recognize the impact your work has on the brand, and, perhaps more important, that the brand SHOULD have on your work, you're being naïve, and you will lose sales in the long run." Sorry, Steve, but that's where you're dead wrong.

As a direct response copywriter, your responsibility is one thing and one thing only: to maximize return on investment (ROI) from every promotion you write. Direct response isn't a branding tool. People barely remember million-dollar TV campaigns. Trust me that they forget 99.99 percent of your mail the minute they toss it. Whenever you subordinate ROI to worrying about "the impact your work has on the brand," or anything else, you are compromising the ability of your promotion to maximize response.

When I sit down to write a letter, I think of only one thing: what true, ethical, and legal thing can I say that will get my prospect to buy this product? And not, "How can I create a good image" or "How does this build the brand?" I have been doing it that way for twen-

26

ty-five years with pretty good results. So, what branding guidelines should direct mail copywriters follow, and which should they ignore? Here are three recommendations you ignore at your peril:

1. Whenever your product has a strong, well-recognized, respected brand, leverage that in your direct mail. For instance, if you are writing a sales letter to sell a new book from Harvard Business School Publishing, the Harvard name and crest should appear prominently as a graphic on your mailer. If you are selling subscriptions to a stock market newsletter from *The Motley Fool*, feature the famous fool icon.

2. Do not force your direct marketing copywriter or agency to use specific branding tag lines, wording, or images in their copy and design. Do not make it a requirement or even a suggestion to follow the branding guidelines. Reason: the minute your creative team begins worrying about anything other than return on investment, you compromise the integrity of your direct mail package and its ability to achieve your primary mission of generating maximum response.

3. Be aware that many branding guidelines, especially bright corporate colors, large logos, and slick graphics, can actually *depress* response to direct mail.

You see, direct mail often works best when it *doesn't* look like marketing communications or advertising and instead more closely resembles a real, personal letter. Adding all the branding stuff can quickly eliminate that edge.

"I can't count the amount of times when a client has given me a list of brand guidelines to follow, and those guidelines have done nothing but stifle response," says copywriter Steve Slaunwhite. "What works in brand communications often doesn't work in direct response. The best you can do for your brand is to sell the product," concludes Steve. "And direct marketing is, or at least should be, indelibly focused on doing just that."

CHAPTER 8

Marketing with Postcards

The standard #10 direct mail package is the workhorse of direct marketing, but after September 11th and the anthrax scare, self-mailers saw a resurgence in other forms, most notably the magalog for long copy and the standard postcard for short copy. Because of limited space for graphics and copy, and lack of a response form, postcards work best when the following conditions exist:

1. The product is familiar to the reader or, if not familiar, simple in nature and easy to explain.

2. The marketing objective is to generate a lead or inquiry, rather than to generate mail orders accompanied by checks and credit card payments.

3. The offer features a premium or other free item the prospect can send for, such as a demo disk, CD, catalog, or brochure.

Why use postcards instead of a traditional direct mail package, tri-fold self-mailer, or other formats?

1. "Postcards offer immediate impact," says Perry Frank of Modern Postcards. The message is immediately visible, with no envelopes to open. "Postcards stand out in the mail with a brief, to-the-point message. Even when someone is sorting incoming mail over the trash can, the postcard will get noticed and read—even if it's on its way to getting tossed."

2. You can bypass lingering concerns about anthrax or other terrorist acts involving the mail. "With the recent anthrax scare, people are leery of opening envelopes from businesses they don't recognize," wrote Sean Lyden on Entrepreneur.com. Furthermore, he noted the envelope is a barrier to your message because you need to convince the recipient to open it and read the letter inside.

3. Creative and printing costs for postcards are much less than for a full-blown direct mail package, because there are no envelopes, letters, brochures, buck slips, or other inserts. The 2006 cost to mail a standard size (4 ¼ by 6-inch) postcard is twenty-four cents versus thirty-nine cents for a one-ounce First-class letter. That's a postage savings of one hundred fifty dollars per thousand.

4. Ease of production. With no folding, binding, or packaging, postcards have only two sides—the front and the back.

5. Postcards offer an affordable option for testing offers and creative prior to launching a more costly campaign. They can also be used to qualify prospects prior to mailing catalogs and other, more expensive direct mail packages. A postcard announcing that a new catalog will be mailing gives the recipient a chance to opt-out from future mailings, saving the marketer production and mailing costs by updating their list.

6. Many postcards wind up on the refrigerator or walls of cubicles in the office, giving them greater visibility and 'shelf life' than regular direct mail. "Mail someone a postcard that really grabbed their attention, and chances are they'll hang onto it," says Frank. Copywriter Roscoe Barnes adds: "Some postcards are collector's items. They are designed to be kept and praised. To work, however, they must have a striking drawing, painting, or photograph. Using the works of a famous artist helps."

7. Postcards are extremely versatile. They can be used for coupons, invitations, announcements, save-the-date reminders, thank-

you cards, follow-ups, special offers, inserts in magazines, admission tickets, mini-newsletters, bookmarks and quick-reference guides.

8. Postcards can drive response to a website URL or toll-free phone number. Add a perforation with a tear-off business reply card to create a 'double postcard,' and you can generate mail response as well.

9. Postcards also offer a quick, affordable way to create clever campaigns with a consistent theme. "We see many of these mailing on a regular basis to the same audience with trivia questions, creating anticipation for the next mailing," says Frank.

What marketers have used postcards with success in recent months? Let's look at five examples.

Case study #1: Haag Engineering Company. Haag Engineering Company specializes in failure and damage consulting; the analysis of why a structure, such as a bridge or building, collapsed. Clients include manufacturers, insurance companies, and law firms. Accredited in several states to provide continuing education, Haag recently mailed twenty thousand postcards to promote their seminars. Recipients of the card are driven to their website to view course offerings and locations. The card can also be kept as a reminder: while visiting a client, one of Haag's engineers saw that the client had the postcard pinned to their wall. Response rates, according to Cheryl Markstahler, marketing manager, average between ten and twenty-five percent.

Case study #2: The USA Rice Federation. The USA Rice Federation is a trade association promoting the eating of rice. They recently mailed a postcard promoting September as National Rice Month to 6,800 food professionals. The postcard offers free brochures, posters, recipes, and other materials, driving response to a phone number or email address. Because the federation is in the business of promoting rice, they have an extensive library of beautiful food photographs in stock, allowing them to produce high-quality postcards inexpensively. With limited staff and budget, postcards are both cost-effective and time-efficient. "Postcards work extremely well in establishing or maintaining relationships and keeping rice top-of-mind among our target audience," says Kimberly Park, Director of National Consumer Education. The postcards generated a response rate of almost three percent.

Case study #3: Coopersmith List Consultants (CLC). Coopersmith List Consultants is a 'boutique' list-consulting firm. They specialize in working with business-to-business marketers who use direct mail but are not direct marketers per se; e.g., industrial manufacturers and technology firms. These companies often need highly specialized niche lists that are difficult to find. But they typically mail in quantities too small to command much attention and personalized service from larger list brokers.

I wrote the copy for this postcard knowing this niche intimately, having come from a background in industrial marketing. The postcard educates these non-direct marketers on basic facts I knew they were unaware of: (1) list brokers exist; (2) they do not charge for making list recommendations; and (3) you do not pay more when you rent the list from a broker versus from the owner directly. This is common knowledge to readers of *Inside Direct Mail*, but a revelation to recipients of the CLC postcard, which told them all these facts and encouraged them to call or go online for free list recommendations.

A previous mailing of one thousand pieces had pulled only two inquiries with no new clients—a 0.2 percent response rate. The new 'educational' postcard pulled two hundred fifty inquiries from a mailing of ten thousand pieces—a 2.5 percent response, more than ten times the previous effort. And more important, many of the inquiries converted into new clients. "The postcard as a format is, by its very nature, short and to the point," says Gail Coopersmith, president of CLC. "It is terrific at uncovering an initial requirement."

Case study #4: Peter Miserendino. Peter Miserendino is an acoustic guitarist who wanted to promote his critically acclaimed CD, "Well-strung & Solo." He believed that sales would most likely come at live performances. To get quality bookings, Peter, who is also a professional illustrator and designer, designed his own postcard and sent it to high-end clubs. Recipients were asked to phone or email for information on booking Peter as a performer. Peter mailed this postcard three times, with three weeks between mail drops. Only three days after the first drop, calls came in inquiring about dates. The same held true for the second drop, and the third, even though the club managers had received the exact same postcard each time. "This confirms that consistency and frequency are a major component of direct mail strategy," says Miserendino. He also attributes his good response rates to the right design, succinct copy, and four-color printing.

Case study #5: Apogee Rockets. Apogee makes model rocket kits for hobbyists and enthusiasts. They did a small test mailing of five-hundred postcards to sell a Saturn V rocket kit. Postcards were printed on a digital press. The back shows a four-color photo of the rocket. On the front, the digital press allowed each card to be personalized. "I wanted to make each postcard look like it was hand-written," says Tim Van Milligan of Apogee. "That's why I selected the font used. I also changed the line spacing on each paragraph, and skewed paragraphs because it would look less perfect."

For the short run of five hundred cards, the digital printing cost one dollar per card. The kits cost two hundred dollars each. Of the five hundred recipients, twenty-five people ordered the product—a five percent response. "Would I do this again? Yes," says Tim. "From the response I got, it appeared that the recipients did think the postcards were handwritten."

CHAPTER 9

What Goes on the Outer Envelope?

It is not uncommon for a marketer to invest a tremendous amount of time, effort, and money in a new direct mail package, and then create the outer envelope almost as an afterthought. That is a mistake, because tests have shown that varying the outer envelope can increase or depress response rates in an *A/B* split—even if the mailing inside is identical—by twenty-five to one hundred percent. Here are nine important outer envelope factors to consider when putting together your next mailing:

1. To tease or not to tease? We use outer envelope teasers because we think the strong teaser we have written will increase response. But there are times when a teaser—even one we think is strong— has the opposite effect and actually *decreases* response. Some marketers argue that the purpose of the teaser is to get the recipient to open the outer envelope. But a blank envelope from a stranger gets opened every time: you want to know what it is and who it's from. So why use a teaser at all? Copywriter Bob Matheo says the function of a teaser is to create a positive expectation for what's inside the envelope. Recommendation: if you can't come up with compelling copy for the outer envelope, don't use a teaser. If you have a teaser you think is strong, do an *A/B* split test of a teaser vs. no teaser. Then roll out with the winner.

2. Who is it from? The corner card—the sender's name and address on the outer envelope—tells the reader who the letter is from. Let's say you are doing a mailing to sell subscriptions to an investment newsletter. The letter could be from the editor (Ron Gurian), the publisher (Capital Financial Media), or the publication itself (*Tech Stock Update*). The corner card copy is not trivial, and should be tested. One publisher had just the name of the editor and the name of the publishing company in the corner card. When they added the name of the publication, it depressed response by twenty-five percent.

3. Company letterhead or plain envelope? When the recipient gets an envelope with the logo of a company he does not know, he suspects that he is getting promotional mail and is therefore less likely to open the envelope, read the contents, and respond. To avoid this happening, you can omit your logo and set the company name and address in the corner card in plain type, such as Helvetica or New Courier.

When your company or brand is well known, using your corporate logo may lift response. IT professionals, for instance, are likely to read a mailing from IBM because they think it may be important technical or product news. A number of mailers type the name of the person who signed the letter in New Courier above the logo, so it looks as if it was typed on the envelope by hand. Those who have done it tell me the technique increases their response.

4. Paper stock and color? In a test, a mailer did an *A/B* split of their control using a kraft envelope versus a white envelope. The white envelope outpulled the kraft envelope by twenty-five percent. This does not mean that the rule is 'white always outpulls kraft.' It *does* mean, however, that outer envelopes matter and you should test.

Agora Publishing's long-time control for *International Living* mailed in a #10 white envelope. When the control threatened to tire, they revived it by taking the entire package, putting it inside a kraft envelope with a cover letter, and mailing it that way.

5. Size? Test different sizes: monarch, #10, #11, #14, 6 by 9-inch, and the 9 by 12-inch jumbo. In direct mail envelopes, size does matter, so this is worth testing. A common result is that the jumbo lifts response over the #10, but not enough to make it profitable. Exceptions? Tons.

6. Stamp, meter, or indicia? Conventional wisdom says that best to worst, in order of preference, is a stamp, then a meter, then a preprinted indicia. Some marketers report a lift in response when using commemoratives and other unusual stamps. Another technique I've seen work with a jumbo mailing is to use multiple low-denomination stamps to reach the total required for postage.

7. First-class or Standard? Direct mail that sells a product via mail-order is almost always sent either Standard or Enhanced Carrier Route Standard because of the economics. However, if you are doing lead-generation mailings to business prospects using just a letter in an envelope with a reply card, and your universe is small, First-class may lift your response.

8. Window? Should you use a closed-face envelope? Or should you use a window envelope? Test. The advantage of a closed-face envelope is that it looks like real personal or business mail. The advantage of the window envelope is that the recipient's name and address can be imprinted or affixed to the reply element, which is positioned so that they show through the window—eliminating the need for the customers to write in their own name and address.

9. Bulk? Should the envelope be flat? Or should you make it bulky, and therefore arouse the reader's curiosity, by putting something inside it other than paper? The marketing director for a national nonprofit told me that all of their best-performing packages have 'heft' created by a small, enclosed object, such as a crucifix or necklace.

When I worked for a manufacturer of wire mesh used in chemical plants, we dramatically boosted response by enclosing an actual sample of the wire mesh along with our sales letter (actually, we designed the letter as a faux shipping tag and attached it to the sample). The teaser on the bulky envelope read, "Your FREE mesh mist eliminator enclosed."

Enclosing an unusual object works especially well when you plan to follow up each package with a phone call. A contractor sent a brick with his business card silk-screened on it. When he called to follow up, he told prospects, "I'm the guy who sent you the brick." He almost always got through.

Part III

Online Marketing

CHAPTER 10

Ten Steps to
Online Marketing Success

"I want to market my business on the web, but how do I get traffic to my site?" one client asked recently. "And if I want to sell my product or service using email marketing, who do I send the emails to?"

Here is an online marketing methodology that has been proven effective for many different types of businesses. The primary concept: *online marketing works best when you email to people who already know you.* Therefore, successful online marketers build their house file or e-list (lists of prospects and their email addresses) using the process outlined below, and then sell to those people via email marketing:

1. Build a website that positions you as an expert or guru in your field. This is the base of operations for your online marketing campaign (see steps 2 and 3 below).

2. This website should include a home page, an 'About the Company' page, your bio, and a page with brief descriptions of your products and services (each product or service description can link to a longer document on the individual item).

3. You should also have an 'Articles Page' where you post articles you have written on your area of specialty, and where visitors can read and download these articles for free.

4. Write a short special report or white paper on your area of expertise, and make this available to people who visit your site. They can download it for free as a PDF, but in exchange, they have to register and give you their email address (and any other information you want to capture).

5. Consider also offering a monthly online newsletter, or *e-zine*. People who visit your site can subscribe free if they register and give you their email address. You may want to give the visitor the option of checking a box that reads: "I give you and other companies you select permission to send me email about products, services, news, and offers that may be of interest to me."

6. The more useful content you feature on your site, the better. More people will be attracted to your site, and they will spend more time on it. They will also tell others about your site. You can even add a feature that allows your visitors to email your articles to their friends—a good idea since it spreads the word about you and your site.

7. The model is to drive traffic to your site where you get them to sign up for either your free report or free e-zine. Once they register, you have their email address and can now market to them via email as often as you like at no extra cost.

8. The bulk of your online leads, sales, and profits will come from repeat email marketing to this house e-list of prospects. Therefore, your goal is to build a large e-list of qualified prospects as quickly and inexpensively as you can.

9. There are a number of online marketing options, which can drive traffic to your site. These include: free publicity; email marketing; banner advertising; co-registrations; affiliate marketing; search engine optimization; direct mail; and e-zine advertising.

10. The key to success is to try a lot of different tactics in small and inexpensive tests, throw out the ones that don't work, and do more of the ones that are effective.

Another question that comes up concerns *frequency*. How often can you send promotional email offers to your house e-list? Every time you send an email to your house file, a small percentage of the list will *unsubscribe*, meaning they ask to be taken off your list. The number of people who unsubscribe is called the *opt-out rate*. Start increasing the frequency of promotional email to your house file. As soon as the opt-out rate spikes upward, stop. You have now reached your maximum frequency.

Many marketers have discovered that the frequency of email promotion to the house file can be much higher than previously thought. Some are successfully emailing different offers to their house e-list as often as two times a day or even more. This is good news for marketers, since the more frequently you can email offers to your list, the more money you can make. Best of all, the profit on these sales to your house file is higher, since the email promotion costs almost nothing because there are no postage or printing costs.

CHAPTER 11

How to Write and Publish an Effective Promotional E-Zine

My monthly e-zine, *The Direct Response Letter* (go to www.bly. com to subscribe or view back issues), is not the most successful or widely read e-zine on the planet. Far from it. But marketing results and comments from subscribers tell me my simple formula for creating the e-zine—which, including copy and layout, takes me just an hour or two per issue to complete from start to finish—works. In this chapter, I want to share the formula with you, so you can produce an effective e-zine of your own, sitting at your computer, without hiring a writer or designer, in just a single morning or afternoon.

If you want to market your product or service over the Internet, I strongly urge you to distribute your own e-zine free to your customers and prospects. There are several reasons for doing so.

First, the e-zine allows you to keep in touch with your best customers—indeed, with all your customers—at virtually no cost. Because it's electronic, there's no printing or postage expense.

Second, by offering potential customers a free subscription to your e-zine, you can capture their email address and add them to your online database. You can then market to these prospects, also at no cost.

Whether you are generating leads or direct sales, there are two ways to sell your products and services to your e-zine subscribers. One is to place small online ads in the regular issues of your e-zine.

These ads are usually a hundred words or so in length, and include a link to a page on your site where the subscriber can read about and order the product. Or, you can send stand-alone email messages to your subscribers, again promoting a specific product and with a link to your site.

When you are dealing with a free e-zine (as opposed to an on-line newsletter which the reader pays for), people spend just a little time reading it before they delete it with a click of the mouse. I am convinced that most subscribers do not print out the e-zine, take it home, and curl up with it on the couch later to read. Therefore, I use a quick-reading format designed to allow the subscribers to read my e-zine online right when they open it. In this format, my e-zine always has between five and seven short articles. They are usually just a few paragraphs each. Every article can be read in less than a minute, so it never takes more than seven minutes to read the whole issue, though I doubt most people do. You can see the most recent issue at www.bly.com to get a feel for the length and content of these articles.

I advise against having just a headline and a one-line description of the article, with a link to the full text of the article. All this clicking forces your subscribers to do a lot of work to read your articles, and that's not what they want. I do not use HTML; my e-zine is text only. This way it is easy and inexpensive to produce. I don't make a production out of it; it's just straight type. Many readers have told me they like it this way, and that they don't like HTML e-zines, which look (a) more promotional and less informational, and (b) seem to have more to read.

When preparing your text e-zine for distribution, type your copy, in a single column, in Times Roman or another easy-to-read type font. The column width should be sixty characters, so you can set your margins at twenty and eighty characters. However, to make sure the lines come out evenly, you must use a hard carriage return by hitting 'return' at the end of each line.

There are a variety of services and software programs for distributing your e-zine as well as your email marketing messages to your online database. I use and recommend Bulking Pro (www. bulkingpro.com). My distribution frequency is monthly, though occasionally I do a second issue if there is major news that month.

I am a freelance copywriter. Let me show you specifically how having an e-zine helps bring in business for me. I recently gave a speech on software direct marketing. It was recorded, so I had audio cassette copies made. In my e-zine, I offered the cassette free to any subscribers involved in software marketing—potential clients for my copywriting services. Within twenty-four hours after I distributed the e-zine, we received over two hundred inquiries from marketing managers at software companies requesting the tape, many of whom needed copy written for direct mail and email to promote their software.

By comparison, most copywriters tell me that when they send postal direct mail to a list of prospects, they average a two percent response. At that rate, they would have to send out ten thousand pieces of mail to generate the two hundred leads I got in an hour for free. That's what an e-zine can do for you. Once you build your subscriber list, you have an incredibly powerful marketing tool and the most valuable asset your business can own: a database of buyers with email addresses and permission to mail to them at any time.

A variety of online marketing tools are used to drive potential customers to a web page where they can sign up for a free subscription to your e-zine in exchange for giving you their email address. You can also ask for their name, which allows you to personalize future emails you send to them.

These traffic-building methods include such things as contextual marketing, banner ads, online ads in e-zines reaching similar audiences, email marketing, pay-per-click advertising, and search engine optimization of the e-zine sign-up website. The acquisition cost per subscriber can range from one to five dollars a name, depending on the method used and the market targeted.

Generally, the larger and more targeted your subscriber list, the more profitable your online marketing will be. After all, a *click-through rate* (CTR) of one percent to a thousand e-zine subscribers will bring just ten visitors to your landing page; but if you have a million online subscribers, a one percent CTR will generate ten thousand visits.

But for your e-zine to work as an online marketing tool, subscribers must not only sign up, they must also open and read your e-newsletters. If they don't open the current issue, they can't respond to any of the ads or offers you make in it. And if they don't read it on an ongoing basis, they will eventually unsubscribe, and you will lose them as an online prospect. In my experience, the best e-zines—those with the highest open, read, and click-through rates—are those that present useful how-to tips in short, bite-size chunks, and the more practical and actionable, the better.

Your e-zine is not the place to pontificate on business philosophy or explain complex technology; you can send your subscribers to web pages and downloadable white papers or special reports that cover those topics. Instead, e-zine readers love practical articles that tell them how to do something useful—and do so in just a few concise paragraphs.

News also can serve as effective e-zine content, but by itself, is not as potent as advice. The best way to use news is to link a tip or other advice to the news. For instance, if you are a financial publisher talking about fifty dollar a barrel crude, tell the reader which oil stocks he should own to profit from rising oil prices.

You don't need a news angle to make advice an effective content strategy for your free e-zine. However, if you can relate your tips to current events or news, do so; experience shows that it can potentially double your readership and response. That being said, you never know what article is going to strike your e-zine reader's fancy. And it's often not the article you'd think. For instance, a manager for a company that sells information on safety to HR managers publishes a regular e-zine on safety and other HR issues. He reports that his best-read article of all time was, "10 Ways to Reduce Eye Strain at Your PC." The eye strain article generated way more response than more specialized articles targeted to his HR audience. Go figure.

Here's what I've found makes the ideal e-zine article (many of these ideas are borrowed from my colleague, Ilise Benun, of www. artofselfpromotion.com):

1. Think of yourself as a conduit. Your job is to pass useful information along to those who can use it.

2. Pay close attention to questions, problems and ideas that come up when you're doing your work or interacting with customers.

3. Distill the lesson (or lessons) into a tip that you can share with your network, via email or snail mail or even in simple conversation.

4. State the problem or situation as an introduction to your tip. Distill it down into its essence.

5. Give the solution. Tips are action-oriented. So make sure you give a couple of action steps to take. Readers especially love something they can use right away, like the article I referenced on how to reduce eye-strain while working at a PC.

6. Describe the result or benefit of using these tips to provide some incentive to take the action. If there are tools they can use to measure the results of your tip once they put it into practice, give them a link to websites offering these tools.

7. Include tips the reader can use without doing any work, phrases they can use verbatim, boilerplate clauses, checklists, forms, and so on.

8. List websites and other resources where readers can go for more info.

9. Give your best tip first, in case people don't read the whole thing, because sometimes even really short tips are too much.

Be aware that most e-zines have a dual audience consisting of: (1) prospects who get the free e-zine but not your paid subscription product and (2) subscribers who have paid for your magazine or newsletter and get your free e-zine as a supplement. For reasons of economy of scale and simplicity of management, most publishers use one e-zine to serve both audiences. But you have to keep the different needs and perspectives of both groups in mind for your e-zine to be effective.

The first group of e-zine subscribers consists of people who have signed up for your free online newsletter. They do not subscribe to your paid subscription magazine or newsletter; and in fact, may not even be aware of it—or you. Your goal with these subscribers is to (a) delight them with the free e-zine they are receiving and (b) upgrade them to the next step—a thirty-day free trial to your paid service. To accomplish these goals:

1. Pack the e-zine with solid content. Nothing beats useful, practical, how-to tips.

2. Put a one hundred word ad in each issue of your e-zine offering a free thirty-day trial to your paid subscription publication, with a link to a landing page where the reader can accept such an offer.

3. Send at least one solo email to subscribers between e-zine issues giving them a compelling reason to accept your thirty-day free trial offer; this could be the offer of a free special report or other premium. Ideally they can get the premium as a downloadable PDF after they register for it on your landing page.

The second group of e-zine subscribers is readers who have already paid for a subscription to your print magazine or newsletter.

Your e-zine can do any or all of the following for your paid sub-scribers:

1. Give them news updates, recommendations, and fresh ideas between monthly print issues.

2. Highlight or expand upon ideas and tips already presented in their print issues.

3. Bring them special discount offers on your other products: periodicals, conferences, seminars, CDs, directories, and whatever else you sell.

Can you stray from my formula of how-to advice and tips? Of course. My e-zine, *The Direct Response Letter,* uses many different types of articles including book reviews, quotations, news items, and new product announcements. But take a tip from me: when you're putting together your next e-zine issue, remember that nothing gains the reader's interest and attention like solid how-to tips.

CHAPTER 12

Build Your E-Zine Subscriber List with *Safelists*

Online marketing expert Debbie Weil recently asked me, "How do you know whether an e-zine is successful?"

"An e-zine is successful if it achieves its stated marketing objective," I replied. "Conversely, if you have no written marketing goal for your e-zine, you have no way to determine whether it is worthwhile."

The original goal of my e-zine was simply to update clients, prospects, book buyers, seminar attendees, and colleagues about things I was doing that they wanted to know about, such as publication of a new book or availability of a recent speech on audiocassette. As a result, I kept it deliberately small: between sign-ups on the home page of www.bly.com and email addresses added from my database, circulation was about two thousand, and that was fine with me. But my plans changed, and I suddenly wanted to get a lot more subscribers in a hurry. One reason was that a larger e-list would mean more sales of my books when announced in the e-zine. In fact, my publishers were concerned that with such a small circulation, sales of my books to my e-zine readers would be insignificant. Also, a larger list would allow me to do cross-promotions with other e-zines, enabling me to reach a wider market for my books and tapes, as well as drive more people to my speaking engagements and website.

I called Peter DeCaro, my freelance web master, and gave him the task of adding new e-zine subscribers. To my amazement, within six weeks he had built my e-zine distribution list from two thousand to more than *sixty thousand* subscribers.

"How did you do it so quickly and inexpensively?" I asked Peter (the entire fee was around one thousand dollars). "Safelists," he replied.

As Peter explained it to me, the Internet users on what is known as a *safelist* have agreed to provide their email address in exchange for the ability to regularly promote to the list's membership. It is known as a safelist, I suppose, because it is 'safe' to send promotional material to these people—they have opted in and agreed to receive it. Peter has joined numerous safelists for the purposes of promoting his clients' offers, including me and my free e-zine. You and I can join, too. There's no exclusivity. Some Safelists are free to promote to; others require a fee. But the fee is a tiny fraction of what you'd pay to mail to traditional rented opt-in e-lists, which can run two to four hundred dollars per thousand.

What works in promotions targeted to Safelists? "Free offers tend to pull well in safelists," says DeCaro. "So by offering a free report or some other freebie in your promotion, you establish credibility with the safelist subscribers and encourage them to investigate the source of the ad—you—further." Some Safelists permit only text ads; others allow either text or HTML. Peter says HTML ads pull better on safelists. I asked Peter where one finds safelists. He recommends several online directories that contain safelist listings, including www.mailpro-network.com, www.megasubmitters.com, www.targetsafelists.com, and www.101-website-traffic.com.

Here's how our promotion worked. Instead of sending safelist subscribers directly to www.bly.com to simply sign up for the free e-zine right away, we first directed them to a special landing page offering a free bonus report as an extra incentive for subscribing to the e-zine. The copy on this landing page began:

"For a limited time, you can get a **FREE** copy of my report offering recession-proof business strategies by clicking here. Apply these techniques to your own marketing and selling efforts during a recession or a down time, and you will survive—even prosper—while others struggle to get by . . . ."

A link at the bottom allowed the reader to click onto my home page to sign up for the e-zine. An autoresponder automatically fulfilled the subscriber's request for the free report. Peter suggests using a cgi-based autoresponder as opposed to a pay service. A cgi script is prewritten code that performs the autoresponder function of automatically responding to email requests. A good website that reviews different cgi autoresponder scripts is www.autoresponder-review.com. Many cgi scripts can be found on www.scriptsearch. com.

At this point you may be thinking that safelists sound like an Internet scam and that the quality of the names can't be any good. This I don't know yet—it's too early for me to tell. I do know that the unsubscribe rate for safelist-acquired names is many times higher than people who subscribe to my e-zine either because they (a) know me or (b) signed up for it on www.bly.com. What I *do* know is that if you're interested in quantity and not necessarily quality, safelists can be an effective way to build your e-zine subscriber base in a hurry at very low cost.

CHAPTER 13

Seven Affordable Ways to Drive Traffic to Your Website

How do you drive traffic to your website without burning through your available cash in a couple of weeks? Here are seven cost-effective ways to get hits to your site:

1. *Google.* The world's largest search engine, Google facilitates 250 million web searches per day for its users. As an advertiser, you can buy preference in Google's search engine, based on key word, on a cost-per-click basis.

It could cost you as little as a dime a click or more than a dollar a click, depending on the popularity of the key word you want to buy. If the cost of the key word is thirty cents per click, and one hundred people click on your site that day as a result of a Google search on the key word you bought, Google charges you thirty dollars. Google lets you put a limit on how much you spend per day, so the cost can fit any budget.

2. *Overture.* Another search engine that lets you buy preferential rating on key words. Overture reaches over eighty percent of active Internet users by displaying your business in search results on leading sites like Yahoo!, MSN, and Alta Vista.

How do you determine what you can afford to pay? Say your product costs one hundred dollars and out of every one hundred clicks on your site, you get one sale, for a total of one hundred dollars. You can afford to pay one dollar per hit if breaking even on the initial sale is your goal.

3. *Affiliate marketing*. Find websites that cater to the same market you do. Arrange for them to feature your products on their site and in their emails. Online ads, email blurbs, and web pages talking about your product link to your site where the user can purchase the product under discussion. The affiliate receives a percentage of the sale ranging from fifteen to fifty percent. To recruit affiliates or to find opportunities to make money being an affiliate for other marketers, visit www.affiliatesdirectory.com.

Amazon.com runs one of the largest affiliate programs, enabling you to feature books on your site that are related to your topic and of interest to your audience; when users click on the book page, they are automatically linked to www.amazon.com where they can then purchase the book online. It's a service for your visitors, and you earn a small commission on each sale.

4. *Co-registration*. In co-registration marketing, the user who visits a website is served a pop-up window containing a number of special offers. Most frequently these are subscriptions to free e-zines. By arranging to have your e-zine or another offer featured in these co-registration pop-ups, you can capture many new names for your online database at a relatively low cost compared with traditional email marketing.

There are a number of companies that can find such co-registration deals for you. One of these is VentureDirect Online, www.venturedirect.com. Another is E-Tactics, www.e-tactics.com.

5. *Banner ads*. Banner ads have seen a resurgence thanks to the increasing sophistication and popularity of Macromedia Flash. In an attempt to recapture the attention of the overloaded Internet user, animation and effects in banners have become more sophisticated and dynamic. Banner ads can work but should be tested conservatively and cautiously, and don't get your hopes of a break-

through up too high. Banner ads usually supplement other traffic generation methods, and are only occasionally a primary source of unique visits. Exceptions? Of course.

6. *Online ads.* Online ads offer an excellent opportunity to minimize costs while generating productive responses. The e-zine publisher specifies the format and length of your ad, which is typically one hundred words of text with one URL link. The higher up (earlier) your ad appears in the e-zine, the higher the response.

7. *Viral marketing.* At its simplest, viral marketing requires adding a line to your outgoing email marketing messages that says, "Please feel free to forward this email to your friends so they can enjoy this special offer." To work, the email you want the recipient to forward must contain a special offer, either a free offer (typically free content) or a discount on merchandise. According to Bryan Heathman of 24/7 Media, eighty-one percent of viral email recipients will pass the email on to at least one other person.

CHAPTER 14

Breaking into the Prospect's
Email Inner Circle

With direct mail response rates continuing to decline, telemarketing impeded by the Do Not Call list, and CAN-SPAM controlling email marketing, direct marketers are constantly exploring channels to find the magic formula that will work for them.

In email marketing, the explosion of spam and the widespread use of email filtering software have depressed click-through rates to new lows. So how can you make email marketing work? According to an article in *The Marketing Report* (October 27, 2003, page 5), a survey by Nielsen/NetRatings found that most people regularly open and read a maximum of sixteen permission-based emails. The only way to break into the inner circle is to displace someone, the survey said. And an article in *DM News* (October 6, 2003) reported, "Marketers will have to enter that emerging inner circle of trusted companies from whom people are willing to keep reading emails." Okay, but how do you break into this inner circle of email senders whose messages your prospects will open and read? It's not easy, but there are six options that seem to work with some level of success:

1. *Free e-zine.* Write and publish a truly valuable e-zine and offer it free to folks who give you their email address. If you publish regularly (at least once a month) and provide content of genuine worth, readers will come to value your publication and establish a

relationship with you. You will have entered their inner email circle, because they will view anything with your name in the 'From' line as being from a trusted advisor and worth their time to at least read and open. A good example of an effective e-zine that generates reader loyalty is Agora's *Daily Reckoning* (www.dailyreckoning. com).

2. *News and updates.* Similar to an e-zine, some publishers send short news bulletins to their subscribers on a regular basis. *ComputerWorld* sends a daily online update with short items from the magazine. You can purchase a short online ad in these updates, thereby buying your way into the reader's inner email circle. CMP, a trade publisher, emails a monthly update, *Business Technology Advisor (BTA),* to the subscribers of all its publications. For two hundred dollars per thousand, you can sponsor *BTA*, having the entire issue devoted to your firm and products. Since CMP subscribers know and look forward to *BTA*, your message gets a higher readership and response than it would if you send it under your own banner.

3. *Service and upgrade notices.* Software users will read and open emails from their software publishers that contain news about upgrades, technical information, or service policies. If your customers regularly need to receive service and product news from you, get in the habit of delivering it via email. Then they will become trained to read your emails, so when you send a promotion, it too will get opened and read.

4. *Transaction emails.* A survey from www.quris.com shows that customers do value and read two specific types of emails: (a) transaction confirmations and (b) account status updates. So you can get your promotional message read by embedding it into routine emails that contain transactional or account status information. A good example is www.amazon.com, whose customers open and read the emails amazon.com sends because they might contain news about their order.

5. *Alert services.* Consumer newsletters, especially investment advisories, have pioneered this approach. When you pay for your monthly subscription, the publisher offers you a bonus: additional content, sent periodically via email, to keep you updated on the topic between regular issues. The catch: you have to give the publisher your email address to receive this free online bonus. The publisher quickly builds an e-list of subscribers who eagerly anticipate and read the emails, because they are viewed as valuable information they pay for as part of their subscription. The most successful publishers keep the information content of the emails high, but also liberally promote products and services to these email alert recipients.

6. *Club or membership.* Your prospects will read emails from clubs, associations, online communities of interest, subscription websites and other organizations of which they are members. Therefore, if you can create a club or have your email distributed by one of these membership organizations, you can enter the prospect's email inner circle.

As a rule of thumb, whenever you can send email to your prospect using one of the above methods, your chances of getting opened and read increase exponentially versus sending a typical promotional email.

CHAPTER 15

The Online Conversion Model for Doing Business on the Internet

We direct marketing types don't give up. When the Internet sprung into life, we said, "Direct mail works offline to sell products via mail order; why not online, too?" So we rented email lists and sent them emails asking them to buy. It bombed. But instead of giving up, we went back to the drawing board, asking, "If traditional acquisition direct response does not work online, let's find something that does!" And that something is online conversion. Both traditional and online direct marketers have tested it, and many are enjoying promising results. In a nutshell, here's an oversimplified version of how online conversion works:

1. You create some free content.

2. You offer people the free content online.

3. When they accept, you then upsell them to your paid subscription product—again, online.

Let's break down each step.

Step 1: Create some free content. This is the easiest step. Just repackage some of your content as an information premium. The content does not have to be long. Re-purposing existing articles works fine for this purpose. So do special reports specifically written for the online conversion campaign. Or the same reports you offer as premiums in postal direct marketing. The premium is typically offered as a "free special report." It is usually available as a downloadable PDF file. Some marketers prefer to post the report as a multi-page html document on the Web.

Step 2: Offering the free content. The most common way to offer the free content is by sending an email to your house file. You can also test outside lists. The email offers the content as a 'free special report.' To get the free report, the recipients click on an embedded URL in the message text. If the content is a downloadable PDF file, the recipients are brought to a short transaction page. They enter their email address, and are then allowed to download and print the PDF file. If the content is a series of sequential HTML pages, the recipients are brought to a short transaction page. They enter their email address, click 'Submit,' and are brought to the first page of the micro site where the report is available to read as a posted HTML document. Tip: within the HTML report, put a number of links to a landing page or transaction page for your paid subscription product. Many readers may click on these links and order your paid product while they are in the middle of reading your free bonus report online. Either way, the reader must give us his email address to read the free report, which is the key to the online conversion method.

There are other methods you can use to generate leads for your online conversion campaign. Some publishers have had great success with postcards; others have used banners or online ads in e-zines.

Step 3: Converting the leads to paid subscribers. Now, two things have happened. First, we have captured the prospect's email address, so we can market to him as often as we like at virtually no cost. And second, we know that the prospect is interested in the topic of our content, because he at least requested a free article or report on it. Since the content was free, we do not know at this point whether he will pay for more content on this topic. But he is a qualified lead in the sense that he is (a) interested in the topic and (b) responds to online marketing.

The next step is to send him a series of emails, known as the online conversion series, with the objective of converting him from a requester of free content to a subscriber or buyer of our paid content. Let's assume in this example we are selling a subscription to a magazine or newsletter, though with modification, the online conversion model can work for tangible products as well.

Planning the online conversion series. While the online conversion process is still relatively new, experience so far shows that our online conversion series works best with between three to seven efforts. Some marketers like every email in the series to attempt to make a sale; that is, they all have a URL the reader can click to reach a page from which the product may be ordered. Others like the first two emails to be simply goodwill, promoting the value of the information and encouraging the readers to actually read the free content—and in some cases, even giving them more free content. These are called *free touch* emails, because they touch the reader without asking him to purchase. Subsequent emails in the series ask for the order; these are called *conversion emails*. In a six-effort series, the first one or two emails might be free touch; the remainder, conversion emails.

Designing the online response vehicle. When the reader clicks on the URL link in your email, he may go either to a landing page or a transaction page. A landing page has a fair amount of descriptive copy about the product you are selling and your offer. It does a strong job of selling the reader on the value of the product. A transaction page has minimal description of the product. It is basically an online order form. Some marketers always send the email recipient who clicks on the link in the email to the landing page, on the theory that the more sales copy there is, the more sales that will be made. Other marketers believe that if the conversion email is long and has a lot of sales copy, there is no need to repeat this in a landing page; and so they just send the prospect to a short transaction page.

<u>Creating the conversion offer</u>. The best offer for an online conversion effort is a free thirty-day trial of the product. If you can set up your site so that the recipient's credit card is not billed until after the thirty-day trial period, that's the best choice. Then you are truly offering a free trial or free thirty-day subscription. By comparison, if you charge their credit card as soon as they submit their order, it is not really a free thirty-day trial; it is a risk-free thirty-day trial. They are paying, but if they cancel within thirty days, they get a refund.

<u>Executing the online conversion series</u>. You can experiment with timing, number of efforts, and mix of efforts (free touch and online conversion) in your series. A typical series might go like this:

Day 1. Email #1, free touch. Thank the prospects for requesting your free content and reinforce its value.

Day 2. Email #2, free touch. Encourage the prospects to read the free content and highlight its value. Point out some especially good ideas, tips, or strategies it contains.

Day 4. Email #3, online conversion. Tell the prospects they can get more of the same content by accepting a free thirty-day trial to your publication. Sell them on the publication and its value.

Day 7. Email #4, online conversion. Remind the prospects that they can still become experts on the topic by getting your publication and accepting your free trial offer.

Day 14. Email #5, online conversion. Tell the prospects the free thirty-day trial is expiring, resell them on the content you are offering, and urge them to act today. Tell them after that, it's too late.

<u>Writing the online conversion series</u>. Write your online conversion series emails the same as you would write other online and offline promotions to sell your products: use the same copy, content, and organization; get attention in the lead; generate interest; create desire for your product; and ask for the order. One key difference: in your lead, always acknowledge that they are hearing from you as

a follow-up to the free report or article they *asked* you to send them. This has two benefits. First, they may feel slightly more obligated to read your message; after all, you did give them a gift. And second, if they liked the free content, it automatically puts them in a receptive mood for more of the same—even if they have to pay for it.

Should you try online conversion? Every publisher who wants to market information products on the Internet should try an on-line conversion series. If you have targeted the right audience for your publication, and the free content you give is of high quality and value, then enough of the readers will want more of the same that they will be willing to accept a free thirty-day trial of a paid subscription product on the same topic. And if your paid subscription product is of high quality and value, a large percentage of the readers will not cancel, and you will have successfully converted free content requesters to paid buyers—your goal in online conversion.

CHAPTER 16

Secrets of Successful
Search Engine Optimization

Recently, I read an article in a marketing magazine advising repeating keywords on your site as often as possible, and in multiple places, so search engine *spiders* can find them. My friend and fellow copywriter, Nick Usborne, says that this advice is not only wrong, but actually harmful.

"This is the worst possible advice you can give to anyone about optimizing their site for the search engines," says Nick. "It's an element of what is referred to as 'keyword stuffing' and is either ignored by the search engine algorithms or, in bad cases, your page and site will be penalized. Worse still, it results in pages that read very strangely to human visitors. Using keywords too often on a page and in the meta-tags is worse than not using them at all. The frequency or otherwise of keywords on a page has nothing to do with whether a spider will find the page. And if a spider finds the page, it doesn't need a keyword repeated frequently in order to find it."

Since I am not an SEO expert, I asked a number of consultants in this area—and others more knowledgeable than me—to comment on the topic of keyword usage on websites.

"I think stuffing keywords on a web page is taking the focus off where it needs to be to be successful in any business," says Sean Woodruff. "That focus should be trained squarely on the customer. Stuffing keywords is a gimmick that is focused on tricking the search engines."

"Yes, search engines are important," says Susan Getgood. "But it is far more important to have a good website that sells effectively. We should focus on writing good copy that effectively communicates the offer. I expect that keywords appear an appropriate amount in good selling copy versus some artificial stuffing exercise which doesn't fool the search engines and likely damages your overall communications effort. Remember, people do land on your website from other sources—advertising, direct mail, and so on—not just from search engines. It is silly to try to optimize for one source, if in doing so, you end up with a sub-optimal website for all the others."

"I often furrowed my brow at suggestions of altering copy to optimize search engine results," says Bruce DeBoer. "It wasn't so much that I knew my way was better, but rather that I couldn't imagine altering otherwise great copy to satisfy a search engine."

Apryl Parcher advises, "When writing websites, it's more important to put keywords in meta tags and descriptions that are only used by spiders, and not seen by the average person reading your page, and also to give your pages titles in HTML that truly reflect the page's contents. While it is true that words are picked up on your home page for the search engine description—unless the text block is made into an image—it's usually the first twenty words or so. So make sure that text is what you want people to see when they pick you up on Google. However, you can go all out in putting appropriate search keywords in your description tags without stuffing your actual copy with them."

"Never stuff a web page with keywords; it's awful advice," says Paul Woodhouse. "You make sure they're in your title and your meta data. Place them carefully in the beginning, middle, and end of your spiel—and in the h1, h2 tags if necessary. Any more than that and you risk being penalized by Google; although you can find many a site getting away with it. Also, it simply reads awfully. But, don't take my word for it. Go to www.seochat.com for expert advice."

"If you want to attract search engine spiders and repel your human visitors, then by all means, stuff away," says Andrea Harris. "Good web writing is a balance between satisfying the spiders and the humans. But it's the humans who buy your products and services."

"It's not about 'stuffing' copy with keywords," says Richard Leader. "It's about making sure the keywords are in there. Some years back, I ran an online training company. Our course outlines were quite clearly course outlines to a human reader, but not to a spider. We realized we didn't once use the phrase 'HTML training course,' for example. So, we added it in a few times—and yeah, it looked a bit clunky. But with just a couple of mentions (for example, 'In this HTML training course, you will learn…'), we increased our search engine traffic—and our conversions. So, my advice is not to stuff but to 'strategically place.'"

"Placing keywords within your site is certainly an important part of getting search engines to notice you," says Joel Heffner. "However, my current favorite way to appeal to search engines is to ping entries that I make to my blogs. Search engines appear to love to run to see what's been added to a blog. If you create a link to a specific page, the search engine will take note of that page as well."

CHAPTER 17

Fourteen Elements of Successful Online Store Websites

A confession: I am not the target prospect for www.bluenile.com, an online marketer of jewelry, because I don't like or wear jewelry (my wife is not a jewelry 'nut' either, and I have two sons and one nephew, and no daughters or nieces). I'm going to try hard to make sure that doesn't color my review of their site.

Let me admit to another prejudice before I start: I don't like complicated, busy, crammed websites. And that's one reason why I was so dazzled by www.bluenile.com: it's a model of effective simplicity for online marketing. The following critique offers an evaluation of the fourteen elements of a successful online website, examining the positive and negative findings for the above-average Blue Nile website.

1. *Brand preference.* The Blue Nile website supports and builds brand preference and encourages return visits. When you click on www.bluenile.com, you are immediately served a pop-up window with an irresistible offer: in return for entering your email address, sex, age, zip code, and marital status, you are entered into a sweepstakes to win a diamond with an appraised value of $5,000. There is a check box where you can opt in to receive offers and announcements by email, but this is already checked off. So you'd have to uncheck it to get off their list.

The home page is cleanly and clearly laid out; in fact, it's almost a little too stark. One could argue a jewelry site should be more elegant in design. But I don't: the jewelry shopper is well served here. At the top is a banner with the Blue Nile logo and the tag line, "Education, Guidance, Diamonds, and Fine Jewelry." It does an adequate job of positioning the site, but it doesn't engage me in a powerful way.

Copy under and to the right of the banner positions the site more effectively: "As the largest online retailer of certified diamonds and fine jewelry, we offer outstanding quality, selection, and value." Interestingly, they make no mention of saving money or time by buying online versus going to a local jeweler.

From there, the home page has pictures of jewelry and product descriptions that are hyperlinked to pages showing and describing those products. Simple and basic, but sensible; I wouldn't do it any other way. There are also three additional value-added links on the home page:

"How to Choose a Diamond Ring" is a useful, informative guide to purchasing a diamond ring.

"Build Your Own Diamond Ring" lets you customize and then order a ring online with the stone and setting you select.

"Diamonds" searches for diamonds based on cut, color, clarity, carat weight, and price.

2. *Strategic intent or purpose.* Blue Nile clearly indicates the action to be taken. The mission of the website—to help the consumer shop for and buy a diamond or other jewelry online—is crystal clear. The entire site is designed to make the transaction as easy and painless as possible. Most of the hyperlinks on the home page go to specific products, so you can see what stones and jewelry are available. These pages are augmented by a useful but not overwhelming choice of some helpful content and functionality—mainly tips on buying diamonds, product searches, and interactive jewelry design.

3. *Content webification.* Blue Nile uses appropriate web-based communication technology. To me, the site uses web-based technology judiciously and appropriately. Sure, you could think of features to add: links to other websites on diamonds; a bulletin board for jewelry buyers to share experiences; the ability to get questions answered via email by a Blue Nile jeweler or gemologist. But it's all unnecessary. The site is not an information resource; it is a place to conveniently buy diamonds and jewelry online. And it fulfills that mission brilliantly.

4. *Relationship building.* Content personalization devices are present on the site. The major personalization feature is "Build Your Own Diamond Ring," which allows the consumer to mix and match stones and settings to personal preference, rather than buy a ring off the shelf. There's not much other personalization, nor is it needed.

One neat idea would be a tool where I could enter the names and dates of major events (birthday, anniversary) for friends and family. Then, when it is my assistant's birthday, www.bluenile.com could send me an email reminder with a gift suggestion. The website does allow you to enter your email address to receive reminders of major holidays, but it is not customizable to your personal list of gift recipients.

5. *Community building.* No community involvement devices are present, a weakness. A website for people with a strong interest in diamonds as collectibles, investments, or gems would be a good candidate for a bulletin board or other community-building device. But www.bluenile.com is a pure shopping site. Yes, www.amazon.com is also a shopping site, and it has the community-involvement device of allowing customers to post product reviews. Could www.bluenile.com do the same? Of course. Is the lack of such a product review feature sorely felt by the jewelry shopper visiting Blue Nile? It doesn't seem so to me.

6. *Persistent navigation*. Blue Nile does an excellent job at letting users fulfill goals. It's fun and easy to shop for jewelry on Blue Nile. You can easily find what you are looking for, the shopping cart works well, and there are always links that let you drill down for more product detail and consumer information, whether it's a close-up photograph of a ring or a schematic diagram showing how a certain setting holds the stone in place.

Navigation isn't perfect: there are some valuable content pages you can't easily find from the home page, and that are only brought to your attention once you're on other pages within the site (e.g., a page explaining how to read independent diamond grading reports). I might expand the menu of choices on the home page to make more of these content pages easier to find when you first log onto the site.

7. *Critical tasks*. The Blue Nile user was able to complete the four critical online tasks: (1) shopping for and finding products; (2) learning more details about products; (3) completing a purchase; and (4) handling customer service-related activities such as reporting a problem with delivery or canceling or returning an order.

8. *Accurate navigational expectations*. The Blue Nile links and buttons do exactly what they say. All links, buttons, and menu choices are clearly labeled. When you click on them, you get exactly what you would expect.

9. *Labeling and language*. Blue Nile is audience-centric and has customer-oriented usage of key words and phrases. The language throughout is suited to the target audience: consumers buying jewelry. Jargon and technical terms are avoided. Everything is simple, easy to follow, and crystal clear.

10. *Readability (content density)*. The Blue Nile website is uncluttered, with adequate white space, pleasing column width, readable type size and face. The page layouts are nearly perfect. Adequate use of white space creates a clean, uncluttered look and

makes the images—photos of jewelry—stand out. You never feel overwhelmed by the text or graphics, and so are inclined to spend more time browsing and shopping, a very pleasant experience.

11. *Organization (marketing quadrants)*. The website's marketing quadrants are appropriately exploited and navigation is good. The home page is divided into classical marketing quadrants. The first quadrant contains a horizontal series of standard buttons hyperlinked to major menu choices (jewelry, watches and accessories) along the top of the home page under the banner. The second quadrant is the series of menu items in the left column, which are headings (diamonds, earrings) that are underlined to indicate a hyperlink. There is some redundancy between these two quadrants. The third quadrant is the main home page space, which has photos and lists of items (products, consumer information, tools), again underlined to indicate a hyperlink. The fourth quadrant is a horizontal series of items at the bottom of the home page, mainly to do with customer service (returns, financing).

12. *Content freshness.* Blue Nile's website update schedule is either infrequent or unclear. There is no information on how often the selection of products on the website is updated, or which items on the site are new, or where to find new items. These are significant shortcomings and offer opportunities for improvement.

13. *Load time.* The site loads in under twenty-five seconds on 56K for text—low graphic load. Tests of the Blue Nile website, using the Web Page Analyzer at www.websiteoptimization.com, took 17.51 seconds to download at 56K. That means it's a fairly fast downloading site, not burdened by overuse of graphics.

14. *Aesthetics.* The Blue Nile aesthetics support the purpose of the site and are consistent with the user's mental model and visual expectations. The design fully complements the function and mission of the site: to showcase and sell high-quality diamond and other jewelry online.

Overall, the Blue Nile website is well above average. The only major addition I would suggest is a page giving the visitor reasons why buying your diamond ring online at www.bluenile.com is preferable to just visiting your local jeweler.

CHAPTER 18

The Needs Assessment Model for Online Marketing

I had mixed feelings when Don Nicholas of the Mequoda Library asked me to take a look at www.ediets.com as my first website review for his publication *Internet Media Review.* The reason is my weight. You know those height/weight charts you see in the doctor's office? Well, according to that chart, I am seven-foot-eight! So, I knew visiting a diet site would be an unpleasant reminder of my ongoing battle to leave porker territory. On the other hand, I'd be going to a site that offered me genuine benefits that I seek—mainly weight loss—a site where I would be a legitimate potential customer. Here, I have added letter grades to further evaluate and quantify the websites on the familiar *A, B, C, D,* and *F* scale.

1. *Brand Preference. Grade: C.* eDiets sends confusing messages or subjugates brand to higher authority. On February 5, 2004, when I first clicked onto the eDiets home page, the main graphic featured a picture of Victoria Principal with some article titles, and it seemed to deliberately resemble the front cover of a women's magazine—in particular, *Lady's Home Journal.* So right away, as a male, I could not relate to the home page. Maybe eDiets is mainly targeting women, but half of the one hundred million or so males in America are overweight, too.

The home page is what I call tabloid style—lots of interesting little items to choose from. Unfortunately, with a tabloid style home page, there's no single point of focus, and no unifying positioning copy to tie it all together or define the brand of the site. Although the large magazine cover graphic catches the eye, I was drawn to an interactive box which said, "Lose 20 Pounds by March 25."

You enter your height, weight, and age and then click through a series of screens asking you more questions so that eDiets can design a customized weight loss plan for you, for which they charge $11.96 a month. Along the way, you are offered a number of free e-zine subscriptions and information on advertised products, which makes it a little bit confusing and overwhelming.

The request for $11.96 a month at the end of the process came as a surprise to me; I somehow thought everything would be free. The reason it surprised me was that there is no selling copy preceding the questioning process. So being asked for money came as a bit of a shock. And I didn't buy. That's just my personal reaction; I have no idea what the actual conversion rate is. Interestingly, when I went to the diet plan questionnaire to run through it again, I was immediately served a page that said, "Welcome back, Bob. We've saved all your information. Click here to view it now. Click here for a special offer for return visitors!" When I clicked on the special offer for return visitors, however, it was the same $11.96 a month I had been offered earlier. I didn't see what was special or different about the offer.

2. Strategic Intent or Purpose, Grade: C. eDiets has too many actions to be taken. There are way too many choices on this site. At first glance, you'd think that's a good thing: lots of valuable content. But unlike sites with a lot of free downloadable content, most of eDiets seems to cost money. So again, it's not quite what you'd expect, as you get asked for a few dollars almost everywhere you go on the site.

If the lead product is the eDiets plan I was offered for $11.96 a month under the box "Lose 10 Pounds by March 25," then I might suggest a split test of the current site versus a product-specific, long-copy micro-site. This dedicated micro-site would center solely on getting people to sign up for the eDiets plan, and eliminate all other content and options. Once people sign up for the eDiets plan, then they can be directed to the existing site—part of which could be password-protected for eDiets plan customers only—where they can explore the other resources such as fitness and recipes.

3. *Content webification. Grade: A.* eDiets features innovative use of interactivity and multimedia technology. The site helps users choose which information program is best for them. Choices include diets, meal plans, exercise programs, and support. The site then communicates with you daily and automatically with emails containing timely, personalized information and inspiration.

There's a lot of interactivity that allows advice to be customized based on age, weight, and body mass index, among other factors, which adds a sense of legitimacy and credibility. After all, how can you give me exercise advice if you don't know how lean or heavy I am, or what kind of shape I am in (oval, in my case)?

A lot of the advice is customized based on your answers to online questionnaires, but the questionnaires are often not designed well. For instance, a Diet Needs Analysis asks me "What kinds of foods can you NOT live without?" The choices are fruits and vegetables; meat, poultry, fish, and eggs; and breads, grains, and cereals. But the system only allows you to choose one category. What if you can't live without both meat *and* bread?

4. *Relationship building. Grade: A.* eDiets clearly invites visitors to personalize website content. Few sites I've seen are more personalized and interactive than eDiets. The content you receive is tailored based on your eating habits, exercise routines, weight, health, and other relevant personal data.

5. *Community building. Grade: A.* The site clearly invites visitors to become involved with other members. At the top of the

home page are buttons that let you select different areas of the site—and community is prominent among them. You are invited to join a community of other health and diet-conscious eDiets users; the cost is $1.99 a week.

6. *Persistent navigation. Grade: A.* eDiets does an excellent job at letting users fulfill goals. Actually, I'd give it an *A* minus. Overall, the choices and pathways are clear, but sometimes the screens are slightly overloaded with offers, ads, and links.

7. *Critical tasks. Grade: A.* Users are able to complete all four critical tasks. There is never a problem in completing questionnaires or going through the steps to get to the offer or content you seek. My primary complaint, as mentioned earlier, is that questionnaire design is not always logical.

8. *Accurate navigational expectations. Grade: A.* Links and buttons clearly do what they say and promise. There are lots of links to a multitude of services and content on the eDiets website, and all links are clearly marked and easily accessible.

9. *Labeling and language. Grade: A.* The website is audience-centric and has good representation of key words and phrases. All terms are in the target prospect's language: weight, exercise, diet, meal plans, recipes, fitness, personal trainer. There's no nutrition or medical jargon of any kind. Everything is written in plain English aimed at a lay audience.

10. *Readability (content density). Grade: B.* eDiets does a reasonable job of balancing graphics to text. The pages are relatively clean and easy to read. In some instances, however, too many options and items are jammed onto the screen, creating a slightly cluttered look. But it never gets confusing, and you can always figure out how to find what you want and what to do next.

11. *Organization (marketing quadrants). Grade: A.* The four marketing quadrants are appropriately exploited and navigation is good. The site is sensibly organized into sections from which you

can choose using either the buttons at the top of the screen or the boxes and sidebars within the screen.

12. *Content freshness. Grade: F.* The update schedule is infrequent or unclear. I can't tell from looking at the site how often content is updated on the website or how much of it changes. But I'm not sure that's a problem here, since the new content is delivered to users proactively via emails for the services they select. So if I follow the strict definitions of the Mequoda Scorecard we use for *Internet Media Review,* I have to pick *F* for content freshness. But I suspect it's better than that, and probably more like a *B.*

13. *Load time. Grade: C.* The site loads in under fifty seconds on 56K for text—moderate graphic load. The site isn't overly graphics heavy, and I don't really see flash or other rich media. On the broadband connection I use, pages download instantly. Web Page Analyzer (www.websiteoptimization.com), however, showed that it takes 31.62 seconds to download the eDiets home page using a 56 Kbps dial-up connection, which rates the site only a *C* for speed on our Mequoda Scorecard.

14. *Aesthetics, Grade: B.* The aesthetics support the purpose of the site, but may confuse the user's mental model. As I mentioned earlier, this is a tabloid-style home page offering a potpourri of offers, pathways, and options. Many successful websites are designed in this manner. However, when you first hit the home page of www.ediets.com, it's not clear what the site operator wants you to do next. If it's to sign up for the eDiets program, which seems to be the primary product, the user is not clearly directed toward that action.

Do layout, colors, and typefaces fit the site's image and purpose? On the day I visited, the main graphic looked like the cover of a women's magazine, featuring the large image of Victoria Principal. Images that were more representative of fitness and diet—for instance, men and women exercising and showing off slim bodies (or even before and after pictures)—would have served eDiets better here.

Overall, eDiets scores a grade of *B+*. It is an attractive site with a lot going for it: interactivity, customization, personalization, desirable content, contemporary graphics, and the promise of some powerful benefits: lose weight, get healthier, look better, feel good, live longer and enjoy life more.

If it were mine to do, I might test the current www.eDiets. com—which seems to offer access to all of eDiets services equally (as well as those of its sponsors)—against a dedicated micro site whose sole purpose was to get people to sign up for the $11.96 a month eDiets plan. Those who sign up for the plan can then be directed to the current site. There, they can explore and sign up for additional services, such as recipes and personal training. There should also be additional content for these paid subscribers, which they can access with their password. Anyone who tries to leave the micro site without signing up for the eDiets program should be served a pop-under Window offering a free subscription to one of eDiets many free e-zines. This would allow eDiets to capture the email address and send a series of emails via autoresponder attempting to convert these free subscribers to paid eDiets plan buyers.

Waterfront Media has developed a series of profitable websites, one of which is eDiets. Another site you should look at is Denise Austin's fitness and health website, www.deniseaustin.com. All of these sites are based around what I call the "Waterfront Model," a business model for e-commerce that Waterfront has pioneered and perfected. Let's look at the model, using Austin's site as the example.

In the Waterfront Model, the home page is the tabloid style home page with lots of interesting tips, items, and factoids. But prominent on the page is a section with an offer—in Austin's case, "Get your complete online fitness plan!"—with a large 'Start Here' button. The primary goal of the site is to get you to click on Start

Here. When you do, you are offered some sort of an evaluation of your problem, as well as a plan or solution, in return for filling in the online questionnaire.

On Denise Austin's site, this is naturally a health and fitness evaluation, since Austin is a fitness guru. The evaluation centers on weight loss, although it touches on other topics, such as exercise. You click through a few screens, answering simple questions and giving some personal information, like how much you weigh now and your target weight. After completing the assessment, you are offered the solution, which is typically customized (or seemingly customized) content delivered online. This is not a free offer, but the first step in converting you into a customer.

Since this is the 'front end' (first) sale, the cost is typically low: just a few dollars a week or month. Once you buy, you get emails offering add-on products, both Austin's and related items. The fourteen point *Internet Media Report* evaluation includes the following points and grades:

1. *Brand Preference. Grade: B.* The site supports and builds the brand but has some shortcomings. One minor problem is that the content seems to assume that you already know who Denise Austin is and view her as a credible, trusted guru in her field. But I think the site could add a little of this credibility on the home page—perhaps a short bio, video clips of Denise on the talk show circuit, images of magazine covers featuring Denise or covers of her best-selling exercise videos. There is an 'About Denise' page, but perhaps a few key items should be condensed from this page and placed at the top of the home page, to immediately build the brand with visitors. The visitors who already know Denise won't be slowed down by these small additions, and will be further sold on using her as their health advisor. Those less familiar with Austin may be convinced, where otherwise, they would just say, "Who's this person?" and click away.

2. *Strategic Intent or Purpose. Grade: A.* The site clearly indicates the action to be taken. The beauty of the Waterfront Model and all websites built using it, including DeniseAustin.com, is that the action to be taken is loud and clear: click on the button labeled 'Start Here!'

3. *Content Webification. Grade: A.* DeniseAustin.com has innovative use of interactivity and multimedia technology. The core of the Waterfront Model used at DeniseAustin.com is the effective use of an interactive self-assessment questionnaire. The visitor must complete the questionnaire before being offered the fitness plan, which has to be paid for. This creates the perception that the site is delivering personalized advice, not boilerplate content.

4. *Relationship Building. Grade: A.* Not only does the site invite you to personalize the content; you are actually not offered the fitness plan until you do so. The site *forces* you to personalize the content, which makes the advice more genuine; how can you help me improve my health without asking questions (as DeniseAustin. com does) about my health, exercise, diet, height, weight, etc.?

5. *Community building. Grade: B.* Community involvement devices are present. The most prominent involvement devices are several free online newsletters addressing various areas of health and fitness. There is also an 'Ask Denise' page where you can post questions and have Denise answer them for you. I could see adding some forums or discussion groups on health issues about which people get emotional and seek information and support: weight loss, diet, exercise, health, and cardiac fitness, as well as others.

6. *Persistent navigation. Grade: A.* The site does an excellent job at letting users fulfill goals. Perhaps I would give it an *A* minus. Overall, the choices and pathways are clear. A few screens are slightly overloaded with offers, ads, and links.

7. *Critical Tasks. Grade: A.* The user is able to complete all four critical tasks: (1) shopping for and finding products; (2) learn-

ing more details about products; (3) completing a purchase; and (4) handling customer service-related activities such as reporting a problem with delivery or canceling or returning an order. There is never a problem in completing questionnaires or going through the steps to get to the offer or content you seek on the Denise Austin website.

8. *Accurate navigational expectations. Grade: A.* Links and buttons clearly do what they say and what is expected by the site user. There are lots of links to a multitude of services and content on the Denise Austin site, with all links clearly marked and easily accessible.

9. *Labeling and language. Grade: A.* The site is audience-centric and has good representation of key words and phrases. All terms are in the target prospect's language: weight, exercise, diet, meal plans, recipes, fitness, personal trainer. There is no nutrition or medical jargon of any kind. Everything is written in plain English aimed at a lay audience, which is what you would expect, given that Denise is a fitness instructor and not a medical doctor or pharmacist.

10. *Readability (content density). Grade: A.* Uncluttered, adequate white space, column width, type size, and face. Again, I would actually rate this an *A* minus instead of an *A*. The pages are relatively clean and easy to read, but in some instances too many options and items are jammed onto the screen, creating a cluttered look. But it never gets confusing, and you can always figure out how to find what you want and what to do next.

11. *Organization (marketing quadrants). Grade: A.* The four marketing quadrants are appropriately exploited and navigation is good. The site is sensibly organized into quadrants and sections. A horizontal bar at the top of the home page gives us clearly labeled, one-click hyperlink access to the major site sections. In the upper right quadrant of the home page, we have the cornerstone 'Start Here' section of the Waterfront Model. There's no mistaking that

the site wants you to click 'Start Here,' and encourages you to do so by (a) offering a fitness plan and (b) promising a number of bulleted benefits (e.g., "shed 1-2 inches from your waist"). In the upper left quadrant, you gain access to 'Ask Denise,' a question and answer section where Denise Austin answers your fitness and exercise questions. In the lower left quadrant, you get a mix of free content: success stories, news ('What's doing with Denise?'), and daily tips. In the lower right quadrant, you are given a window where you can buy some of Denise's new videos and related fitness products online.

12. *Content freshness. Grade: B.* New content is available daily. As mentioned in #11 above, the lower left quadrant contains daily tips. There is another feature with updated content (a single tip of the day) here called 'Today's Deniseology.' Through these, the site always features fresh content in a place where it's clearly identified as such and is easy to find.

13. *Load time. Grade: C.* Under fifty seconds on 56K for text—low graphic load. Tests of loading time at www.websiteoptimiza-tion.com, revealed the Denise Austin website took 36.61 seconds to download at 56K. With a high-speed Internet connection, you breeze through the site and its functionality without delay.

14. *Aesthetics. Grade: A.* The aesthetics of the site support the purpose of the site and are consistent with the user's mental model. The primary graphics are various images of toned, fit, slim, attractive Denise Austin in exercise clothes, clearly communicating that (a) the site offers help with fitness and exercise, and (b) the methods used obviously achieve the results desired (at least for Denise). Copy on the site indicates that it is aimed at women (for instance, it talks about reducing your dress size). If men were an equal target, I could see using more photographs of Denise and other fitness competitors in slightly more revealing exercise outfits. Not only does sex sell, but such outfits clearly show the tone and fitness achieved.

Overall, the Denise Austin site is graded *A*. The Waterfront Model has been proven to make money selling content online, and has been refined and tested by Waterfront Media in several of their websites including Dr. Andrew Weil, The South Beach Diet, and The Zone Diet. The Denise Austin website is a superior execution of this proven online business model.

CHAPTER 19

Maximize Landing Page Conversion Rates for Search-generated Traffic

The Mequoda Library guidelines outline twelve characteristics a landing page needs to successfully close sales online. And to incorporate all twelve characteristics for a consumer product, typically requires medium to long copy on that landing page. But should you send your traffic directly to that long-copy landing page? Or will visitors be put off by its length? Here is a rule of thumb to follow: when you are generating traffic from an e-zine ad or solo email sent to your e-list, you are reaching an audience 'trained' to read your stuff, and you can send them directly to your long copy landing page. But when you generate traffic through Google Adwords and other pay-per-click advertising, or through organic search, those visitors have much less familiarity with you and no demonstrated inclination to read long copy on your subject.

So for pay-per-click and search traffic, many successful Internet marketers use a two-step landing page process. You are first sent to a relatively short landing page requiring you to enter your email address and continue to read more and get more information. Once you enter your email address, you are taken to a traditional long-copy landing page selling the main offer. An example of this two-step landing page approach is www.taxloopholesoftherich.com. It promotes an information product aimed at consumers on how to save money on your taxes.

When you visit the URL, you see a relatively brief landing page with a headline and six bullets promoting a free CD, which you have to enter your name and email address to receive. When you click, you are taken to a longer landing page where you are told how to get the free CD and are given two options for doing so. Here is the evaluation for Tax Loopholes for the Rich using the Mequoda Library guidelines.

1. *Headline (strategic intent). Grade: B+.* The long landing page has a strong multi-part headline that (a) briefly gives the author's credentials, (b) presents a strong testimonial up front, (c) has a headline, "Stop Over Paying Your Taxes and Throwing Your Money Away," and (d) is followed by a subhead making a big promise—that the product is guaranteed to reduce your taxes by $10,000 or more and also offering $547 worth of free bonus gifts.

The headline offers big benefits in an interesting and compellingly stated offer. The only reason I rate it a *B+* instead of an *A* is that it's missing a sense of urgency: there's little reason to order now instead of later, aside from the vague, not-very-credible claim "quantities very limited." And it would be easy to add a real sense of urgency. You could put a time limit on the offer for the free bonus gifts, or remind the readers that they have to put these tax-savings strategies into action *now* if they are to reduce their next tax bill. If they wait, they misses out on the tax savings for the year.

2. *Story and content. Grade: B.* The content is strong, presenting a coherent argument on why you are paying too much in taxes, why you need this product right away, and how it can reduce your tax payments and put more money in your pocket. Long, specific testimonials with photos of satisfied customers help convince the reader that the product does what the copy says it can do.

The story is not quite as strong. The promised theme is "Tax Loopholes of the Rich," and the copy could have been made much stronger by telling a believable story of why rich people pay less taxes because they take advantage of loopholes others don't, and how the product can help you benefit from these same loopholes even if you are not rich. But this story is never told, and so the 'big idea' behind this promotion—"Tax Loopholes of the Rich"—is never fully exploited.

3. *Content webification. Grade: B.* The copy has been well adapted for the Web through the use of images, layout, and typography. The free bonus CD has a graphically attractive cover, and this image is repeated throughout the landing page to stimulate visitors to click through to the order page.

4. *Email capture. Grade: B.* If you enter this online promotion through the short copy front-end landing page, you must enter your email address to read further and go to the full sales letter on the long-copy landing page and order the product. When you attempt to leave without doing so, you are served a pop-under that says, "Wait!" and once again makes the offer of the free CD. The pop-under contains a button you can click, "Order Now," that takes you back to the order page. But it does not ask you to enter your email. No fallback offer is made (e.g., a free bonus report) in exchange for just the email address.

5. *User Testimonials. Grade: A.* The page has numerous strong, specific testimonials with pictures of satisfied customers.

6. *Links to order flow. Grade: A.* The sequence of events is clear, logical and easy to follow: (a) you go to the front-end short landing page and enter your email address; (b) you click to the long copy landing page; (c) click to the order page where you can order the product, choosing from one of two offers; and finally (d) you are taken to the transaction page where you can buy the offer you selected using your credit card.

7. *Labeling and language. Grade: B+.* Throughout the promotion, the language is in terms that online shoppers understand and respond to, for example, "Order Now," "Yours Free," "Enter your

name and email address to get your free CD that will quickly change your financial life."

8. *Readability and content design. Grade: B.* The entire sequence of pages—front-end short-copy landing page, main long-copy landing page, order page—is clearly laid out and easy to read. All pages also have the publisher's snail mail address and toll-free phone number, further enhancing credibility.

9. *Content freshness and urgency. Grade: C+.* The landing page is powerful but if there is a flaw, it is the lack of content freshness and urgency. To increase content freshness, you could add to the section "you will become aware of" a few bullets referencing important new changes to the tax code. To add a further sense of urgency, see my comments in section #1 of this review about an expiration date for the offer—a deadline by which you must respond to get the free bonuses—or stressing that you will lose tax benefits unless you implement the strategies in the program in a timely manner (e.g., by the end of the current calendar year).

Here's another technique that could add a sense of urgency to this site: put a counter at the top of the long-copy landing page that shows the countdown (number of days) until one of the two significant tax deadlines: December 31 or April 15.

In tiny type at the top of the long-copy landing page it says, "Quantities are limited." But do you really believe it? The product is a CD, and if they run out, can't they just burn more copies? If you say quantities of an information product are limited, you have to make that claim believable by explaining why this is so (e.g., "we have a limited supply, and once the inventory is gone, we will not be going back to press").

10. *Load time. Grade: B.* This is a fast-loading website. When tested on WebSiteOptimization.com, the front-end, short-copy introductory landing page downloaded in just 1.67 seconds over a 56 Kbps connection.

11. *Aesthetics. Grade: B+.* The copy is clearly laid out, and the type is large and easy to read. The landing page makes good use of relevant graphics, including showing an image of the free CD to stimulate orders and photos of satisfied customers next to their testimonials. What other visuals could possibly have been shown? Maybe images of big tax refund checks from the IRS, or a head shot of the product author.

12. *Order options. Grade: A.* The long-copy landing page asks for the order several times throughout the page, showing an image of the free CD with a caption urging the visitor to order: "Get Your FREE CD Now! Tax Loopholes of the Rich! Yours Absolutely Free, Without Commitments, or Obligations." This is accompanied by prominent buttons labeled "Order Now!" So the landing page is working hard to get you to click to the order page. On the order page, you have two options for ordering. The first option sells you a "Wealth Accumulation" program for $47.99, which includes the promised "Free CD" as a bonus. When you click on this option, you go to a clear, easy-to-use transaction page where you can order using your credit card. The second option enables you to get just the CD for free as promised, although there is a $5.94 shipping and handling charge, which means the promoter is still making a sale and getting your credit card information.

This site uses a really strong promotion: good layout, good graphics, great copy, attractive offer. Overall, it is graded a *B+*.

If most of your traffic is generated from search engine optimization or pay-per-click traffic—and not email marketing to your house e-list or online ads in your e-zine—then you may want to test a two-step approach like this versus sending your visitors directly to your long-copy landing page. And if you want to set up a two-step promotion with a short up-front landing page followed by a long-copy traditional landing page, www.taxloopholesoftherich.com provides a great model for you to follow and adapt.

CHAPTER 20

How to Sell E-Books Online

Before the Internet, there was a niche in mail order marketing that involved selling books on how to get rich in mail order. The audience was primarily composed of business opportunity seekers. Now the Internet has created an equivalent market of people who want to get rich on the Internet, and an equivalent niche: selling e-books on how to make money writing and selling e-books.

Most of these e-books are specifically on how to make money on the Internet, and deal with various aspects of selling information online. A few are on more general marketing and selling topics. A small minority deals with subjects outside of business and business opportunities, such as how to buy a home with no money down.

The e-book business model works as follows: You write an e-book on a topic of interest to your potential buyers (Internet millionaire wanna-be's) and format it as a downloadable PDF file. Next, you write a long, powerful sales letter to sell the e-book and post it on the Web as a micro site. Unlike conventional websites, which have a lot of buttons and clicking options, the only thing you can do on a micro site for a single e-book is read the sales copy and, if interested, order the product. E-books are typically covered by a thirty-day money-back guarantee. Even though the product can't be physically returned, anyone who says they are dissatisfied gets a refund. Finally, you drive traffic to the e-book site through a variety of promotional methods, including ads and articles in other people's e-zines, announcements in your own e-zine, banner advertising, co-registrations, cost per acquisition (CPA) deals, affiliate deals with other online marketers, and sending emails to your house file (renting a traditional opt-in list does not typically work for e-book offers because of the high cost).

An affiliate deal involves arranging with other online marketers to sell your e-book to their audiences in exchange for a cut of the revenue ranging from thirty to fifty percent. "Affiliates are my most successful method of selling e-books," says Joe Vitale, author of numerous e-books, including the best-selling Hypnotic Writing, which can be found at www.hypnoticwriting.com. Vitale recommends searching the Internet for online marketers who sell other people's products on their site.

"Recruiting people who buy your e-book and love it is the best way to get affiliates," says Fred Gleek, an online information marketer (www.seminarexpert.com). Include a section in every e-book explaining how the buyer can become an affiliate and sell your e-book to his audience.

"With a new e-book, your own list represents the absolute best way to sell a whole lot of e-books really, really fast," says e-book author Jim Edwards, "People who have bought from you before are highly likely to buy again."

The model for this genre of 'how to get rich online by selling e-books on how to write and sell e-books' is *e-Book Secrets Exposed* (www.ebooksecretsexposed.com) by Jim Edwards and David Garfinkel. Edwards makes a handsome living writing and selling e-books; he has sold more than 5,000 copies of various e-book titles ranging from $29 to $49 over the last twelve months. Keep in mind that the manufacturing and shipping costs for e-books is zero, which is what makes them such an attractive, profitable information product. "I have two e-books that each generate $10,000 to $12,000 gross each per month," says Edwards. "Another does

$3,000 per month in sales, and two others generate $1,200 per month each. One e-Book sold $43,000 in thirty days."

What topics works best? "Topics that address an urgent need that the prospect is aware of, and that you can market to pre-formed Internet groups of prospects," says Garfinkle. "These groups are usually composed of e-zine subscribers and are affinity groups that spend a lot of time on a single website, or discussion groups that allows production promotion." He says that e-books on marketing and big-ticket consumer item topics (e.g., how to negotiate the best price for a car, or how to buy or sell your house) work well.

And what won't sell in the e-book marketplace? "Informative, even valuable topics around which there is no pressing need most of the time," says Garfinkle. He recently advised another online marketer not to go forward with a planned e-book for junior executives on how to sell their ideas to others. The reason? He couldn't find an interested community on the Web of junior managers that have spent money on career-improving topics. "Also, except in rare situations, most junior managers don't feel urgency about selling their ideas to others," David notes.

A word of caution to the buyer: Some e-books are quickly compiled, poorly researched, recycled trash, and a rip-off of their $19 or $29 selling price. Reason: the barriers to entry in e-book marketing are so low anyone can do it. And so the market is flooded with thin PDF documents written by amateurs hoping to make a quick buck. Your best bet if you want to buy and read marketing e-books: buy from the proven authors mentioned in this article: Jim Edwards, David Garfinkel, Fred Gleek, Joe Vitale, as well as other known experts in entrepreneurial online marketing including Terry Dean, Corey Rudel, Jeffrey Lant, and Jim Straw.

CHAPTER 21

Search Engine Optimization
Tips and Tricks

Because so many websites crowd the Internet, you need to make an extra effort to get yours noticed. One way to attract attention is to make your site search-engine-friendly, that is, to increase the odds that search engines will find your site.

There are two key steps that can help you do this. First, submit your site to directories such as Yahoo! and The Open Directory. Second, make your website findable by search engines that send out *spiders* and *crawlers* to scour the Web. Some of the information those spiders and crawlers seek can be found in meta tags"—words or phrases embedded within the HTML code used to create websites. Before you create your own tags, it's a good idea to take a look at those of others, especially competitors and colleagues. You can easily open a window and view the meta tags of any website you visit. From your browser's tool bar, simply choose the 'View' menu. Then click on 'Source,' and a window will open with HTML text that you can study. The most important meta tags are found near the top of the page in between codes like this: <head> and </ head>. If you are creating your own website, depending on which software you use, all you have to do to add meta tags is type the words you've chosen in the appropriate places.

The key meta tags for marketing purposes are title, description, and keywords. These tags control what surfers see when your site is listed in the search engines, which means they will help people decide whether to visit your site. *Title* is what your visitors see at the top of their browser windows when they are visiting your site, as well as what they will see in their bookmark lists. Make sure each page has a title that makes sense to visitors, not just to you. Be descriptive. Failure to put strategic keywords in the page title is often why web pages are poorly ranked.

When your website comes up in search engine findings, the meta tag identified as the *description* is often the opening statement people will use to decide whether to access the link. The description should concisely answer the question, "What do you do?" For example: "XYZ Design provides client-focused, creative and effective graphic design, art direction, and project management for marketing communications."

Keywords are the terms your prospects and visitors will type into the search field when they are looking for talent. So consider the words and phrases they might use to describe your services. Put these keywords in your meta tags. You also should include your keywords in the first twenty-five words of your home page. Here are some additional tips for selecting keywords:

1. Use plurals for your keywords, but avoid excessive repetition.

2. Misspell keywords if misspellings are common. For example, DIRECTV, a digital satellite television service, is frequently referred to as Direct TV. If your name is misspelled regularly, include that spelling in your keywords as well.

3. Don't always use obvious keywords. Include phrases that may get fewer searches but higher results.

4. Don't let your combined keywords exceed 1,000 characters. The fewer keywords, the greater impact they will have.

Maintaining a high ranking in search engines is a time-consuming process. And even with diligence, these efforts may not get you into the top thirty listings, particularly if you're competing in a niche with well-established and better-financed competitors. The best strategy is to register with the major search engines and free directories, and supply your information every time you find a site that offers a free listing. Have a seven-word description ready to copy and paste as well as ten keywords. Devote a certain amount of time each month to maintaining your listings in databases and directories.

I had always thought a good strategy for making your website easy-to-find was choosing a domain name that is clearly descriptive of what you do; e.g., http://www.divorceonline.com if you are a divorce lawyer. But Heather Lloyd-Martin, a copywriter specializing in search engine optimization, disagrees. "This doesn't really work," she says. "Plus, it encourages people to come up with those terrible domains like www.make-money-online-with-internet-marketing.com, which are spammy and are usually downgraded in the engines." She also downplays the importance of tags. According to Martin, "The search engines key on the content—so that's what's important. The title is also important for positioning and conversion off the search engine results page."

If you want search engines to find you, avoid flash or frame pages. "Search engines can find flash or frame pages, but it's harder for them," says Heather. "Fast has indexed Flash for a long time now, but it can be horrid for usability, and it won't gain the best rankings. HTML is truly the best bet."

Portions of this chapter are adapted from *The Online Advantage*, written by Ilise Benun for The Creative Group (www.creativegroup.com).

CHAPTER 22

Guerilla Marketing on the Internet

There are two types of marketing in the world today: (1) *traditional* marketing with its relatively larger budget and reliance on standard methodology and mainstream media, and (2) *guerilla* marketing, which is reliant on non-traditional tactics, alternative media, and such tools as bartering and negotiating to cut costs to a minimum.

In offline direct marketing, traditional usually means sending either a solo direct mail package or a catalog to a house file or rented mailing lists. Guerilla direct marketing in the offline world, by comparison, can involve anything from a package insert and bill stuffer, to per inquiry advertising and late-night TV spots on cable.

In online marketing, traditional marketing usually means banner ads or emails sent to rented e-lists of opt-in names. *Cost per thousand* (CPM) for these opt-in lists is typically one hundred fifty to four hundred dollars per thousand. Guerilla online marketing, by comparison, seeks to generate inquiries, make sales, and build files of online customers through *cost per acquisition* (CPA) deals, banner exchanges, e-zine advertising, e-list swaps, affiliate programs, co-registrations, search engine optimization, and other low-cost methods.

Cost per acquisition means you pay for every name that the email adds to your house file. These names are captured when a recipient clicks through to your landing page, registers, and hits 'submit.' The prospect may be ordering a product, or simply signing up for a free e-zine or special report.

"The idea in email marketing is to acquire new names for the lowest possible cost per name," says Sarah Stambler, president of E-Tactics, an e-marketing agency (www.e-tactics.com). In this regard, CPM can be expensive. Let's say you send out one thousand emails and have paid two hundred dollars to rent the names. Out of the one thousand people, two percent (twenty) click through to your landing page offering a free whitepaper. If ten percent of those click-throughs convert to a sign up, you have acquired two new names at a cost of one hundred dollars per name.

By comparison, some email marketing agencies and consulting firms are arranging CPA deals for their clients. Here the marketer pays a fixed rate per name acquired. For one client, Stambler acquired fresh business-to-business leads at five dollars per name on a CPA deal. However, she says that CPA deals can be tricky to arrange, and many e-list owners are not receptive.

Al Bredenberg, publisher of EmailResults.com, an online marketplace for opt-in email marketing, agrees, although his site does list a number of CPA providers with contact information. "You have a much better chance of convincing e-list owners to work on a CPA basis if you can offer a track record of conversion rates established through previous promotions," says Bredenberg. "List providers are hesitant to take a risk on an unproven product."

Offering the e-list owner a piece of the acquisition in a cost per order (CPO) deal can also work. "You need to offer the list owner a generous revenue share in the range of twenty-five to fifty percent of each order," says Al. "A very low price point doesn't stand much of a chance, unless you can prove conversion rates are very high." Stambler says offering five to eight dollars per order on a forty-dollar product is in the right ballpark.

Another tactic favored by guerilla email marketers is co-registration. This is where a web surfer goes to a site for one offer, such as a free e-zine, and is shown other, usually similar, offers that can also be signed up for at the same time. "Cost for co-registrations varies," says Stambler. "At Lycos, you can pay two to three dollars a name. Sweepstakes sites charge fifty cents a name or so." The nice thing about co-registration deals is that they can be tested on a small budget. For instance, if the cost is fifty cents per name, a two thousand dollar investment will bring you four thousand new names.

Cost per click (CPC), where the marketer pays for every person who clicks through the embedded link in the email message to the landing page, is also available. But Stambler warns against it. "Cost per click is too expensive." If you pay ten cents a click and get one thousand clicks, you are charged one hundred dollars total. But if only two people sign up, your cost is fifty dollars a name.

CHAPTER 23

Blogging for Marketers

Here's a question I've been curious about lately: should marketers add blogging to their arsenal of marketing tactics? Will it help sell more products and services? Or is it an utter waste of time, as I suspect; a pure vanity publication that won't pay you back even one thin dime for your effort?

First, a definition. "A blog is an online journal," explains blogging expert Deb Weil in her Business Blogging Starter Kit (www.wordbiz.com). "It's called a journal because every entry is time and date stamped and always presented in reverse chronological order." The theory is that if you are an information marketer or if you publish information to establish your expertise in a niche industry or field, blogging should be part of your publishing arsenal. According to Deb, a business blog is "a platform from which to lobby, network, and influence sales. It's a way to circumvent traditional media and analysts. And blogging can be done instantly, in real time, at a fraction of the cost of using traditional channels."

Now here's my hesitancy in recommending blogs as a marketing tool: I have yet to find a single marketer who says that a business blog has produced a positive return on investment (ROI). I know plenty of online marketers who make millions of dollars a year from their websites and e-zines, for instance, but I've not seen a blog whose creator says that the time and effort spent on their blog has directly put money into their pockets.

"I would say that, with few exceptions, blogs are not yet direct income producing resources in and of themselves," says blogging authority Paul Chaney (www.radiantmarketing.biz). "Their value lies in the fact that they help raise one's stature relative to their respective field."

In my observation, there are two major problems with blogging as a business-building tool. The first is that most of the blogs I encounter are rambling, streams-of-consciousness musings about a particular topic of interest to the author, largely bereft of the kind of practical, pithy tips that e-zines, websites, and whitepapers offer. As Deb says, reading the blog is like reading the author's journal or diary. And unless you are a guru or celebrity whom others worship from afar, people are simply not going to flock to your blog to discover your latest thoughts on life.

The second problem with blogs is one of distribution. With an e-zine, once the reader subscribes, he gets the e-zine delivered to him electronically every week or every month or however often you send it. But with a blog, the reader has to go out and proactively look for it. And since your contributions to your blog may be irregular and unscheduled, he has no way of knowing when something new of interest has been added.

One big advantage of blogs, according to Paul Chaney, is that having a blog can help pull traffic to your website. "The search engines, especially Google, love blogs," says Paul. "You'd be amazed at how many of your posts will end up in the top ten returns. If search engine optimization is a concern to you, blogs are the best way I know to move up the ladder as well as increase your page rank."

"I confidently predict that blogs will soon be a key piece of an effective online marketing strategy," says Deb Weil. "Ultimately, they're nothing more than an instant publishing tool, one that makes posting fresh content to the Web within anyone's reach. No tech skill or knowledge required." And that's another one of my complaints with blogs in particular and the Web in general: the ease with which people can post and disseminate content. "The best thing about the Web is that anyone can publish on it; the worst thing about the Web is that anyone can publish on it," a computer magazine columnist once observed. The problem is that there is already too much content, and we don't want or need more. Analysis, wisdom, insight, advice, strategies, ideas—yes. But raw information, data, or content—no. And from what I can see, blogs serve up almost none of the former, and tons of the later.

Blogs are, by virtue of being a form of online diary, like diaries: rambling, incoherent, and more suited for private thoughts than public consumption. If you have something of value to share, there are many better formats for doing it online than by blogging, including whitepapers, e-zines, and websites. Even bulletin boards are interactive, so they have value by virtue of shared opinions, dialogue, and engaging conversation which may be listened to openly and publicly. But most blogs seem to be the private idiosyncratic musings of an individual, without censure or editing of any kind. And the result is like porridge: a gloppy mess, tasteless, and not very satisfying. Until that changes, I can't see starting and maintaining a blog of your own, unless you are bored and looking for something to do, or require an outlet for self-expression. And if the latter is the case, why not just buy and keep a diary instead?

When I first published the above in a *DM News column*, I apparently offended a segment of the blogging community by suggesting that perhaps blogs might be "an utter waste of time; a pure vanity publication that won't pay you back even one thin dime for your effort." Here's what all the hoopla has taught me so far: bloggers are a tight-knit community that sticks together and are rabidly enthusiastic about their medium. Many are self-described blogging 'evangelists.' Their attitude toward new and untested marketing media and channels is probably a lot different than yours and mine (I assume that you, like me, are a direct marketer). I told virtually every blogger who said I had treated blogging unfairly the following: "We direct marketers only care about one thing in marketing: return on investment. Unless a dollar spent on a marketing test returns two or three dollars in revenues, we consider that test a failure—and cut off the promotion." For instance, there are direct marketers generating millions of dollars a year in direct product sales from e-zines and email marketing campaigns. One I know produces upwards of forty million dollars in annual sales from their email marketing. I challenged the bloggers: "Can anyone out there show me even a single blog that produces one percent of that—just four hundred thousand dollars in annual sales?" No takers, so far. Not a single blogger could produce evidence of a blog generating a significant, positive ROI (the cut-off figure for which I have chosen direct sales of four hundred thousand dollars a year or more).

But what my challenge *did* produce was a bunch of passionate responses explaining to me why blogging is without question the next big thing in marketing despite its lack of discernible ROI. "It's all about the conversation," writes Marc Orchant, feeding me *The Cluetrain Manifesto's* party line. "That's the point of the blog space. As a lifelong marketer myself, I find the direct marketing industry behind the curve, generally speaking, when it comes to embracing disruptive technologies." Reader B.L. Ochman says, "Blogs help develop a conversation between a company and its customers [and] have become an important part of the marketing mix." As direct marketers, I'm not sure our primary objective is to embrace disruptive technologies or have conversations. Isn't it more about boosting response, generating a positive ROI, and beating the control?

"My argument is that blogging is more likely to raise brand awareness, but that the impact on direct sales will be more difficult to assess," says Max Blumberg. "Therefore, I don't think it is appropriate to look for a close relationship between blogging and direct sales."

Some of the writers who contacted me were eager to compare blogging to direct mail and show me that direct mail is inferior. Blogger Yvonne Divita states, "The small business owner cannot hope to create and support a continuing successful direct mail campaign." I'd recommend Yvonne start reading *DM News*. Every issue is packed with stories of businesses large and small making healthy profits with both traditional direct mail as well as email marketing. Yvonne also told me that when she was a corporate assistant to the CEO of a good-sized company, "I threw all the direct mail in the circular file at my feet. The CEO didn't want to see it. So, who's really reading your client's direct mail piece?" Yvonne seems unaware of the concepts of cost per thousand and break-even analysis, which let us direct marketers make a healthy profit even if ninety-eight out of one hundred prospects toss our mailings away without a second glance. She comments, "When a direct mail piece can only assure the sender of approximately a two percent to three percent return, you can't convince me the hundreds or thousands spent on it is worth it." Tell that to Omaha Steaks, Covenant House, and Phillips!

Jennifer Rice explains that comparing blogs with direct marketing is to look at blogs from the wrong angle: "Blogging is not a direct response vehicle. It's an awareness, visibility, and promotion vehicle that happens to be terrific for those of us selling intellectual capital. It's also extremely useful for corporations to use as a means to connect with customers and get feedback."

Finally, a couple of resources to help you learn more about blogs (I recommend both highly). First, Deb Weil's "Business Blogging Starter Kit," available at www.wordbiz.com. Deb is a blogging evangelist, but her kit contains a lot of useful how-to guidance for anyone thinking about starting a blog. Second, get B.L. Ochman's special report, "What Can Your Company Do With a Blog." Like

Deb's, it is detailed, specific, and instructional. Available at www.whatsnextonline.com.

Recently Ms. Ochman asked me, "Do you still think blogs are baloney?" I replied: "I never thought or actually said they were baloney. I just said that, as a direct marketer, I don't think blogging—a medium with unproven ROI and uneven quality—is something we should get excited about, as the blogosphere has. I think members of the blogosphere should be applauded for their pioneering spirit, but their evangelical enthusiasm is not yet supported by results."

I'm still highly skeptical about the whole blogging thing, and I find the majority of blogs to be lacking in quality and content (to be fair, there are many exceptions here). But I do think the topic warrants further investigation on my part, which includes starting my own blog at www.bly.com/blog.htm. I'll keep you posted and report periodically in my *DM News* columns (posted on www.bly.com) and, of course, on my blog.

Part IV
Subscription Marketing

CHAPTER 24

Six Common Reasons Why Newsletters Fail

Newsletter publishers have been taking a beating in the market-place as of late, with failed launches and weak tests outnumbering the success stories. Direct mail isn't working as well as it used to, and most publishers have not figured out how to profitably acquire new subscribers on the Web. To increase your chances of success, here are the most common reasons why newsletter ideas and promotions don't work—and one good way to overcome each:

1. *Lack of a Big Idea.* With so many information sources today on virtually every topic, why create yet another? To establish its place in the market, your newsletter must have a clear 'reason for being'—a reason why it should exist and why people would want to buy it, even though other publications already exist. What's the 'big idea' behind your publication, the unique selling proposition (USP)? For *FORBES Nanotech Report*, a financial newsletter, the reason for being is to help investors (the audience) increase their profits (the benefit or what it does) by buying shares of emerging nanotechnology companies early, then holding on for large gains (how it does it). If you can't clearly identify the audience, the benefit, and how you achieve the benefit differently than other information sources, then your product lacks a strong USP. And if the USP is weak, no promotion, no matter how strong, is likely to work.

2. *Bad fit.* You may have a clear promise or big idea, but what if it's not something the reader cares about? Then you are doomed to failure. In his 1960 best-seller, *Reality in Advertising*, Rosser Reeves identified the three factors needed to have a strong, effective USP:

(1) Each advertisement must make a proposition to the consumer. Each advertisement must say to the reader, "Buy this product, and you will get this specific benefit."

(2) The proposition must be one that the competition either cannot, or does not, offer. It must be unique—either a uniqueness of brand or a claim not otherwise made in that particular field.

(3) The proposition must be so strong that it can pull in new customers for your product.

The third item above means that the big promise must be a good 'fit' with your audience; something they care about and want. What does your audience really want? You can make an intelligent guess, but you really don't know. That's why smart publishers do *A/B* split tests comparing different USPs, themes, or creative approaches. Often you can test selling propositions inexpensively online with split tests of emails and landing pages, with one set reflecting sales appeal *A* and the second based on sales appeal *B*. If *A* is the winner, then a small direct mail test based on concept *A* would be the next step. If that works, roll-out follows.

3. *High dispensability.* Bombarded by information overload, today's subscribers are less loyal and more ready to discontinue rather than renew. Only those publications that they either (a) really, really like or (b) feels they really need are likely to make the cut in acquisition or renewal decisions. At a meeting of the Newsletter and Electronic Publishers Association (NEPA), I gave a talk entitled "How to Make Your Newsletter Indispensable." Among the tips suggested:

(1) List the URLs of websites where readers can go for more information on your topic.

(2) List valuable resources, such as mini-directories of vendors (with contact information) that can meet subscriber needs.

(3) Focus on news you can use. Don't just give facts, present actionable ideas and information.

(4) Include tools the readers can use verbatim, e.g., boiler-plate clauses that can be inserted into contracts.

To receive a free copy of my "How to Make Your Newsletter Indispensable" seminar on audiocassette, call Fern Dickey at (201) 797-8105 and ask for tape #833. Or email Fern at dickeybf@aol.com.

4. *Soft editorial.* Hard news publications are inherently less dispensable than how-to newsletters. In a pinch, an executive with a beer company can give up a favorite newsletter on leadership, but that person is going to keep the fax or online service giving the daily wholesale pricing on hops and barley. If your content is of the how-to variety, perhaps it is too general. Instead of merely giving tips that sound good, present coherent strategies and proven techniques for solving specific problems. Case histories and success stories are especially useful for making ideas seem more real.

5. *Insufficient return on investment.* If you can prove to the readers that the information and advice in your newsletter will save or make them many times more than your subscription fee, your chances of a sale or renewal are greatly increased. The best strategy is to deliver a rapid return on investment, so that the reader's investment is paid back with the very first issue, in the subscription premium, or even in the promotion itself. For instance, the outer envelope for a promotion for a tax newsletter promised the reader an immediate $6,480 tax savings, and the technique was given on page one of the sales letter.

6. *No depth of reader familiarity.* The best newsletters often have a 'clubby' feel. They are written in the voice of one insider or industry member talking to another. When the editor is an outsider, the newsletter often lacks this authoritative voice. And readers don't trust it. Two solutions:

(1) Hire editors who come from the industry or profession you are writing about.

(2) Have non-expert editors spend time in the field—visiting factories, attending industry events, interviewing experts and subscribers, one on one.

The conclusion? With the glut of information competing for the reader's time and attention, the 'free information' culture created by the Internet, and increasingly limited corporate budgets, you have to offer extraordinary value to your subscribers. That means major benefits such as time savings and rapid return on investment—and ideas, analysis, or information they cannot easily get elsewhere in a digestible, convenient format. That is quite a challenge, but worth taking when you consider that the average newsletter costs the subscriber twenty to fifty times more per page than a magazine on a similar subject (a one hundred page monthly magazine with an annual subscription rate of twenty dollars costs less than two cents a page versus a twelve-page monthly newsletter with an annual subscription rate of one hundred dollars costing more than sixty-nine cents a page).

CHAPTER 25

Make Your Newsletter Indispensable to Your Subscriber

As Bill Bonner, founder of Agora Publishing is fond of pointing out, nobody wakes up in the morning, taps his or her significant other on the shoulder, and says, "Honey, let's go out and buy some newsletters today." People may read books or magazines for entertainment, but they rely on newsletters to deliver tangible value far in excess of the subscription price. How then do you make your newsletter indispensable (or at least less dispensable) to your subscribers—the one publication they must have, even if they let all their other subscriptions lapse? I put the question to a group of successful newsletter publishers and marketers. Here are a few of their answers.

1. Generate a tremendous ROI (return on investment). The more benefits subscribers get from the newsletter, the less likely they are to grumble about your high subscription fee at renewal time. "Find ways to make your product worth many times the subscription price in money generated, cost savings, time savings, freedom, peace of mind, fun, energy, and inspiration," advises one publisher.

2. Make your credibility beyond question. Subscribers who have faith in the editor, writers, and publisher stick with the newsletter. "The information source must be someone I respect as an expert in their field," says one subscriber. "Never let the customer down," advises John Forde, a copywriter with Agora Publishing. "We stick with people because—net-net—they honor the trust we have placed in them."

Business-to-business newsletters can establish credibility by closely aligning themselves with major associations in their industry. "Partner with a high-profile industry association," advises Tom McCaver of Melcrum Publishing. "As long as editorial integrity and independence aren't compromised, you can be seen as the industry mouthpiece and significantly increase your standing in the market."

3. *Avoid the 'information trap.'* Too many promotion packages boast about the 'information' the newsletter delivers. But that's the last thing people want. We're already drowning in information. And we can get all the information we want on the Web for free. What newsletter subscribers want is actionable ideas: savvy strategies; techniques that work; 'news you can use;' and analysis and interpretation.

Tip: Consider publishing case histories. "I meet with many Fortune 1000 CEOs and senior executives, and almost without exception their first question is, 'So what's my competition doing?'" says management consultant David Frey. "People want to know how other people have solved the same problems they are facing and what the post-implementation results were."

4. *Appeal to the reader's self-interest.* As has been observed many times, everyone is tuned to the same radio station in their heads: WIIFM—"What's In It For Me?" When marketing a business-to-business newsletter, don't just show how the publication benefits the subscriber's company by increasing profits, boosting productivity, or controlling costs. Go beyond these by showing how doing these things helps the subscribers advance in their careers, earn more money, and make their jobs more secure. Give subscribers what they want, not just what they need. According to copywriter Parris Lampropolous, "The newsletters that get read first and the ones that have the highest renewal rates are the ones that deal with interests and hobbies."

5. Differentiate yourself from all other competitors. Being different or unique is a powerful strategy for acquiring and retaining subscribers. "The secret is to provide something that no one else can provide," says publisher Buddy Hayden, "or short of that, to provide a rare something which you do demonstrably better than anyone else."

"You've got to make the information you present each month seem like they've never heard it before," says Sandy Frank, an investment newsletter publisher. "You've got to find a way to present copy that seems different than everything else they see in their mailbox."

6. Give the subscriber an incredible value. Infomercial producers know they get more orders when it looks like the viewer is getting a lot of stuff for his or her money. The same technique can work in selling newsletters. "If you are not in a specialized vertical market, I have a feeling that adding ancillary products and services is the best way to make yourself indispensable to the subscriber," comments Brian Kurtz of Boardroom. "Offer extra bonuses or benefits that would cost as much as the subscription price but are offered for free as part of the subscription," advises another consumer newsletter publisher.

The most common premium in newsletter publishing is a free special report. But paper is cheap, so why not offer several reports, each on a different topic of vital interest to your subscribers? Free information premiums can be packaged in many different media, including directories, software, CD-ROM, audiocassettes, video tapes, and resource guides. Thanks to the Internet, you don't even have to print your ancillary products. Increasingly popular in newsletter publishing is including access to a subscribers-only website as part of the subscription. Another common technique is to send supplemental emails alerting subscribers to important news that takes place between regular issues.

7. Prove that the value far outweighs the cost. Copywriter Mike Pavlish says that a critical step in closing sales is making the customer perceive that the price you are asking for your product is a drop in the bucket compared to the value it delivers. One way newsletter publishers do this is by comparing their newsletter to more costly information resources. *American Speaker*, a loose-leaf service for executives on how to be a more effective speaker, compares its $297 annual subscription fee to the $5,000 a professional speechwriter would charge for just one speech. Another technique is to restate the price in terms that make the cost seem more reasonable. By dividing its $297 subscription fee by 365 days in a year, *American Speaker* tells readers that they get continuous advice on how to be more effective speakers all year long for a very reasonable fee of only eighty-one cents a day.

To sum it all up:

(1) Make the information in your newsletter different, unique, useful, and difficult to get elsewhere.

(2) Include content that delivers tangible benefits, such as cost savings or increased profits.

(3) Show that the value of what you deliver to your readers is a drop in the bucket compared to the price you are asking.

CHAPTER 26

Marketing Newsletters in the Information Age

We are now well into the Information Age, and the rise of the Internet has only accelerated the proliferation of free information. The resulting information glut and increasingly rapid access to online content create an especially challenging environment in which to sell subscription newsletters and other high-priced information products.

Theoretically, information products should be the easiest and most profitable items to sell online. Information is virtually the only product that can be delivered electronically over the Internet. A paperback book ordered on amazon.com has to be packed and shipped in the physical world. But a newsletter can be converted to a PDF file and sent electronically as an attachment to an email. Production and shipping cost: zero. Profit margin: high. Yet, in reality, newsletter publishers have met with extremely limited success marketing their publications online. Why is this so? Here are three reasons.

First, although the Internet today has become accepted as a medium for commerce, this was not always so. The Internet originated as a non-commercial medium for the exchange of scientific and technical data. Next, through online services such as CompuServe and Prodigy, the Internet became a medium for personal communication. Marketers began experimenting with the promotion of products in unsolicited emails and in newsgroups, meeting with sporadic success and frequent flaming. Attorneys Martha Siegel and Larry Canter made a splash (not positive) in the Internet community as early spammers; they marketed immigration services online. Next, permission marketing came onto the scene, and it became OK to advertise a product to someone on the Internet as long as they had agreed to let you. So although commerce has become an accepted practice on the Internet, it is still not palatable to many users who believe in strict rules of netiquette. Traditional hard-sell subscription marketing is unfamiliar to, and not universally accepted by, the online community.

Second, the culture of the Internet is one of free and open information exchange. To hardcore Internet users, the idea of paying for content is both alien and repugnant. "Information should be free" the Internet people claim—a position directly in opposition to our objective, which is to make money selling information. Worse, a visit to the Internet shows that information is indeed free. Thousands of individuals and organizations have been bitten with the website bug: the desire to put up a website offering free information and communication about a dazzling array of topics ranging from options trading to *Star Wars*. And they seem happy and eager to do this without financial compensation of any kind.

Third, the proliferation of websites offering free information over the Internet is part of a broader trend: information overload. Our prospects are bombarded by a sickening glut of content that threatens to overwhelm them. Everyone today has too much to read—and not enough time to read it. We in newsletter publishing are fond of pointing out that we save our readers time, rather than take their time. One sales newsletter, for example, boasts that its editors "spend more than eighty hours a month combing through hundreds of sales training programs, books, articles, websites, e-zines, videos and audiocassettes for the most practical, powerful and immediately useful sales ideas and techniques—saving you hours of research time." A common promotional claim for business-to-business newsletters is "Reading time: just twenty minutes a month." But prospects don't always see it this way. When they get your direct mail package, their knee-jerk reaction is, "Oh, no. Not *another* subscription offer. Another publication is the *last* thing I need," and they toss our carefully crafted message aside.

We're also fond of pointing out that we're not just another source of data, but that we convert data, through analysis, into meaningful information and actionable ideas. But consumers again don't often see us this way, and you should question whether your newsletter really lives up to that promise.

What's a newsletter publisher to do? One option is to give up trying to charge for your information. Give it away for free, and try to operate with a model in which the revenue comes from advertising, not subscriptions. There are success stories here, but they are relatively few and far between. One of the big winners is TechTarget, which publishes nineteen e-zines on various topics of interest to Information Technology (IT) professionals. The e-zines are free; TechTarget makes its money from advertising, for which they charge over one hundred dollars cost per thousand (CPM).

If you're an old-fashioned information marketer, and want people to pay for the words you produce, here are some suggestions for staying profitable in today's market:

1. *Get the money up front.* Get a check or credit card with the order. If you want your offer to seem softer, get the credit card information, but don't charge the subscription fee to the card until the trial period is over. Joe Karbo invented this technique decades ago in his "Lazy Man's Way to Riches" ads. The copy promised not to cash the customer's check until the trial period was over and, if he wasn't satisfied, Joe would mail back the check uncashed. Jay Abraham used a similar technique in marketing high-priced boot camps. Instead of cashing your check, he would bring all the checks to the seminar and leave them in a pile on a table in the back of

the room. If you were not satisfied, you could just pick up your uncashed check and go home. Because most of us sell information that is valuable but not absolutely essential, it's too easy for a 'bill me' customer to not pay up when the invoice comes. By getting the money up-front, the whole question of pay-up rates is eliminated before it starts.

2. *Use more generous guarantees.* The standard guarantee in newsletter subscription promotion used to be a thirty-day risk free trial. If you were not satisfied, you could cancel within thirty days, get your money back, and keep the issue or two that you received. After that, you couldn't back out. Faced with declining response rates, newsletter publishers improved their guarantee. Some offered a ninety-day risk-free trial. Others went further: If you canceled within ninety days, you got all your money back. If you canceled after that, you got a refund on the unused portion of your subscription. Now a tight marketplace and tough competition have pushed newsletter guarantees to the highest level possible: the unconditional lifetime guarantee of satisfaction. If you are not satisfied, you may cancel at any time (even on the last day of your subscription), get all your money back, and keep all issues and bonus materials received, in effect, ripping off the publisher.

3. *Short-term trial offers.* At $259 for a one-year subscription, the weekly *Dow Theory Forecast* is relatively expensive as far as general stock market newsletters go. To overcome price resistance, they offer the option of a three-month trial subscription for $79. The idea is to eliminate sticker shock caused by a high purchase price. Online information marketers do this by offering subscriptions on a monthly basis as well as an annual basis.

4. *Demonstrate a rapid return on investment.* For most business subscribers, profits are the bottom line. A $795 a year monthly newsletter seems outrageously expensive. But as sales trainer Brian Tracy points out, the easiest way to sell a $300 product is to show

the buyer how he is getting $1,000 in return. So if you can prove that your $795 a year newsletter can save or make the reader an extra $75,000 a year, price becomes less of an obstacle. If you don't demonstrate a clear return on investment, closing the sale becomes that much more difficult.

5. *Narrow the focus.* Since the rise of the Internet, people are less willing to pay for general information, since so much of it is available free. Salon.com has largely failed because the home page of any search engine gives the same kind of information for free. But people will still pay for highly specialized information they cannot easily obtain elsewhere. The more specialized your niche, the more indispensable your publication to your readers. Focus on 'have to have' information for a specific audience, rather than 'nice to have' or 'interesting to read' content for a general audience.

CHAPTER 27

Finding the Right Offer

When creating a direct mail promotion, the closing copy, especially the offer, often gets short shrift. The marketer simply picks up the boilerplate from previous promotions, without thinking through whether the offer and its wording make sense. And often, they don't. More and more we see offers that are confusing, deceptive, unfair, or illogical, if we look carefully. A number of publishers, for instance, offer lifetime guarantees. They permit the subscriber to cancel at any time and receive a prorated refund on un-mailed issues. But if you offer both a 'bill me' option as well as payment with order, such a lifetime guarantee actually gives the customer an incentive *not* to pay up front—the opposite of what the marketer desires.

Say the customer checks the 'bill me' option for a monthly newsletter, gets his first issue, and then writes "cancel" on his invoice. The publisher doesn't send him a bill for one issue, nor does the publisher ask for the newsletter back. So the customer gets a free issue. But if the customer pays in advance, then cancels after the first issue, he gets a refund for $11/12^{th}$ of the subscription price (the eleven un-mailed issues) and therefore ends up paying for the issue received. Why should the bill me customer get a free issue, but not the payment with order customer? It doesn't make sense, considering a cash with order customer is more desirable than a bill me order. How can you fix this problem? Offer a full money-back guarantee within the first thirty days, then a prorated refund there-after. That way, everyone gets the first issue free if they decide not to become subscribers, whether they enclosed payment with order or chose the bill me option.

The wording in lifetime guarantees is at times ambiguous, un-clear, or even misleading on such offers. The old standard used to offer 'a prorated refund on the unused portion of your subscrip-tion' or on 'un-mailed issues.' No problem there. You knew that if you cancelled after six months and the newsletter cost one hundred dollars, you would get fifty dollars back.

Now many of these guarantees offer "a *full* refund on the unused portion of your subscription." Are they offering one hundred per-cent of your money back? No. By 'full,' they mean the full amount of the cost of the un-mailed issues. Again, for a one hundred dollar subscription cancelled after six months, that's a fifty dollar refund. If you really are giving back the subscribers all of their money, make it clear, e.g., "We'll refund your entire subscription fee in full" or "We'll refund every penny you paid."

Another gray area is the offer of a free issue. Many subscription promotions with a thirty-day money-back guarantee promote the first issue, sent within thirty days, as a free issue. In reality, that issue is free only if you do not become a subscriber. If you do subscribe, then you are paying for that issue, i.e. for a monthly publication, that first issue is one of a total of twelve you will get as part of your one-year subscription. So for those who pay and do not request a refund, there is no free issue. In that case, 'free issue' is not wholly accurate. More correctly, we should say 'risk-free issue' or 'no-risk issue.' To make it a true free issue, you'd have to give them the first issue plus, if they subscribe, twelve more issues—a total of thirteen issues for the price of twelve. Very few newsletters do that, but if you have a how-to newsletter, you could, quite easily. Just create an evergreen 'first issue' and include it in the welcome kit. Then begin their regular subscription with the next issue mailed.

Those of us who use premiums know the danger of offering a too-generous premium with a bill me option: The subscriber responds, gets the premiums, cancels, pays nothing, and keeps all the great free gifts. The solution is to phrase the bill me option check-off box this way: "Bill me (bonus gift sent upon receipt of payment)." The subscribers can still (if they wish) pay, get the bonus, cancel within thirty days, get a refund of that payment, and keep the premium. But that's going to a lot of trouble to get a free special report. Asking for the money before you send the premium gains more of a commitment from the subscriber resulting in fewer replies from people who have no intention of subscribing but just want something free.

At least two publishers have approached me recently with the idea of offering a best-selling book on the topic covered by their publication as a premium. Popular books are a bad choice, however, because many of the people receiving your mailing may already own the book. You could offer a choice of an alternate premium, and ask the subscriber to pick one—either the book or another item. In theory, it sounds good, but it seldom works. The reason is the old rule of thumb: the more choices you ask the buyers to make, the more they have to think about it. And a decision deferred is a decision not made.

The typical guarantee offers a full refund if you cancel the service or return the product within thirty days, but some experts suggest a longer period. How long? Some recommend a lifetime guarantee. Boardroom offers a full refund on the full subscription price, even if you cancel on the last day of your subscription. "It is a great selling point," says Boardroom's Michael Feldstein. "And since very few people cancel on a bill me offer after they pay, the risk is minimal."

CHAPTER 28

What Subscription Premiums Work Best?

Offering one or more premiums is a standard ploy in direct mail used to sell newsletter subscriptions. But what premiums work best? What are your choices? Well, most premiums for newsletter subscription marketing are print products, typically special reports. These include:

1. *The super-premium.* A super-premium is a special report that delivers all or most of the information, secrets, or strategies promised in the mailing piece. Example: a magalog for Weiss's *Safe Money Report* offers a super-premium, "Grow Up to 1,000% Richer in the Great Stock Market Panic of 2002," that delivers on the big promise of the mailing. The offer of the super-premium is made on just about every other page of the twenty-four page magalog.

2. *The owner's manual.* An owner's manual advises the subscriber how to use the service for maximum results and benefits. An options trading course, for instance, will typically have a premium explaining terms (e.g., puts versus calls) and the types of trades the service makes (e.g., straddles).

3. *The vertical premium.* A vertical premium is a report covering in depth one specific area the newsletter deals with rather than the bigger picture. A newsletter on Information Technology, for

instance, might have a special report on supply chain management (SCM) or enterprise resource planning (ERP).

4. *The resource guide.* A resource guide is a mini-directory of vendors, suppliers, associations, websites, and other resources of interest to the newsletter's target audience. Be sure to include addresses, phone numbers, email addresses, and web URLs for listed resources.

5. *Surveys.* The results of subscriber surveys are of great interest to potential subscribers. When *Hospital Admitting Monthly* added the offer of a salary survey premium, response to its control jumped fifty percent.

6. *Best of's.* If you have a regular column that is highly popular with subscribers, collect a dozen of them or so in a 'best of' premium. Newsletters covering regulatory or legal issues have done this with monthly columns on court cases and their outcomes (e.g., The Best of "You Be the Judge").

7. *The editor's magnum opus.* Be careful of offering a book by the editor as a premium, especially if the book is a best-seller or the newsletter is expensive. If the book is a best-seller, many potential subscribers will already own it. If the newsletter is expensive, you're better off offering a premium with a higher perceived value than a book.

The next category of premiums is online or electronic. You may already offer your subscribers information online. Consider positioning some of these online services as premiums.

1. *E-zines.* If you send weekly email updates between monthly print issues, talk about the 'free e-zine' they get as a bonus for subscribing.

2. *E-Alerts.* Some newsletters offer periodic, unscheduled emails when there is important news or instructions that cannot wait for the next print issue or e-zine. If you do this, position it as a value-added premium service.

3. *Online archives.* Access to your password-protected, subscribers-only website is a bonus for subscribers to your print or online newsletter. One feature subscribers look for is an online archive of back issues. If they are searchable by key word, even better.

4. *Forums and chat groups.* Hosting a forum, chat group, or other online community where subscribers can network and share best practices is another nice little online extra. Reading the postings is also great research for your marketing and editorial people.

Here in no particular order are some other premiums newsletter publishers have used with varying degrees of success:

1. *Telephone hotlines.* Many monthly newsletters offer subscribers a telephone hotline they can call to hear current news and advice. Hotlines are typically updated weekly.

2. *Conference invitations.* You can offer potential subscribers invitations to exclusive conferences, workshops, and seminars. They should get these invitations early, before the general public, and a subscriber's discount on the registration fee wouldn't hurt either.

3. *Transcripts.* Transcripts of conferences, seminars, speeches, lectures, even TV or radio appearances by the editor can make attractive premiums.

4. *Audio and video tapes.* You can tape your editorial staff when they give presentations and offer audios or videos as premiums. Videos have a higher perceived value. I prefer audiotapes or CDs because busy people can listen to them in the car.

5. *CD-ROMs.* A CD-ROM can present multimedia material that's difficult to reprint in a printed report. The CD-ROM that comes with my book *Public Relations Kit for Dummies*, for example, includes samples of video news conferences.

6. *Software.* At least one financial newsletter I've seen recently includes trading software as a premium for new subscribers. Software has high perceived value. Is there a simple spreadsheet, such

as a cost calculator, you can put on a disk or CD-ROM and offer as a premium?

7. *Three-ring binders.* For a newsletter that has lasting shelf value as a reference, you can offer a free three-ring binder the subscribers can use to store all their issues in one convenient location.

8. *Merchandise.* Merchandise, a common premium for magazine subscriptions, is seldom used in newsletter promotions. There are rare exceptions. *Release 1.0,* a technology newsletter aimed at high-level decision-making executives, offers a *Release 1.0* baseball cap as a payment with order premium.

CHAPTER 29

Five Most Common Subscription Marketing Mistakes and How to Avoid Them

The glut of free and low-priced information competing for our subscriber's limited time and attention today means we have to work harder than ever in our promotional copy to prove that our newsletter delivers tangible value far in excess of the subscription price. Yet, most newsletter promotions fail to convince most of the potential subscribers reading them of the value of what we are selling. Here are five common errors that, if avoided, will help you convince more of the people on the mailing lists you rent to try your publication.

1. *You haven't explicitly stated the publication's reason for being.* The reason for being is the reason why the publication exists and, by extension, why anyone would want to pay for it. Masthead tag lines usually fail to identify this reason for being. One newsletter, *The Reseller's Report*, advertised itself as "marketing, sales, and management strategies for computer resellers." The niche and content are clear, but not the reason for being. There is a ton of marketing, management, and sales information available today, for resellers and everyone else. Given the easy availability of that information, why do I also need *The Reseller's Report*?

Your reason for being, in addition to identifying the audience and content, must also state a benefit the reader gets from subscribing, preferably one that cannot be found elsewhere. For Phillip's

California Technology Stock Letter, the reason for being is to enable subscribers to earn "four times the return of the S&P 500" by investing in a certain class of stocks that perform well regardless of the market.

2. *You haven't proven your case.* When I say I can help you make four times the returns of the S&P 500, your first reaction is disbelief, followed by, "Prove it!" Copywriters too frequently make claims (e.g., "We give you the news first," "Our analysis is superior") without giving proof, often because digging for that proof is hard work. One way to prove a claim is with specific, detailed examples. A package for *Jane's Defense Weekly* made the claim that *Jane's* provided analysis of defense news more accurate than other sources. The package lead began:

> Iraqi armored personnel carriers lay in smoldering ruins on the battlefield. The newspapers casually referred to these vehicles as "Russian tanks."
>
> But a *Jane's* military analyst knew better, and <u>our</u> article—quite correctly—identified the vehicles as Chinese in origin.
>
> A trivial point? Hardly. In his article, our analyst explained that the Iraqis regard Russian tanks as the finest made, and Chinese the worst.
>
> Conclusion? Iraq didn't consider that battlefield strategically critical, because they were sending their second or third division, not front-line troops.
>
> And knowing this, Iraq's enemies could plan their counter-strategies more effectively.

3. *You haven't established your credibility with the reader.* A classic ad for McGraw-Hill began: "I don't know you. I don't know your company. I don't know your product. Now—what was it you wanted to sell me?" As a high-priced newsletter, you are claiming insight, expertise, knowledge, analysis, or reporting above and be-

yond what the subscriber can get from less expensive sources—the web, newspapers, magazines, trade journals, TV, radio. Your copy must work hard to make the reader believe that your editor, publication, or company is capable of delivering it. In its package, *Jane's Defense* Weekly pointed out that the company has been a leading information resource covering the defense industry for over a century. But the copywriter, in reviewing videos of TV stories involving *Jane's*, came up with a much more powerful credibility builder which he used as an envelope teaser:

> *60 Minutes* calls it "the closest thing there is to a commercial intelligence service—available to anyone with a subscription."

This comment was made by a voice-over TV announcer as the lead-in to a short *60 Minutes* piece on the defense industry in which *Jane's* was featured.

4. *You don't understand what your buyer really wants.* Go beyond the description of your market printed on the list broker's data cards. Ask yourself: Who are these people? What do they believe? What are their feelings? What do they want? What are their attitudes and principles? By incorporating your answers to these questions into your promotional copy, you can reach your prospects on an emotional and personal level, not just an intellectual and logical one. For instance, Information Technology (IT) professionals often have an adversarial relationship with users. A seminar company built a successful promotion around these feelings. The letter headline read, "An important announcement for every IT professional who has ever felt like telling an end user, 'Go to hell.'"

5. *You haven't shown that you're a good investment.* It is not enough to have a strong reason for being, prove your case, establish your credibility, and deliver the benefits your subscriber really wants. You also have to show that the value of those benefits outweighs the rather hefty subscription fee you are asking folks to pay. In other

words, you must show that your price is a drop in the bucket compared to the value the subscriber receives. One way to make this case is to demonstrate a strong return on investment from a subscription to your publication. For instance, a package for a newsletter on personal productivity—*Your Personal Productivity Coach*—stated its reason for being as the ability to save the subscriber at least an hour day through improved personal productivity. The package pointed to a survey showing the average executive's time to be worth sixty dollars. It then calculated that saving one hour a day for five days a week for fifty weeks a year at sixty dollars an hour equaled fifteen thousand dollars gained in increased productivity per employee per year. That's a 100:1 ROI on the $149 annual subscription rate.

CHAPTER 30

How to Market Subscription Information Products Online

A colleague recently said to me, "No one has found the winning formula for selling subscription newsletters online yet." I disagree. A number of publishers—including Agora Publishing and 21st Century Investor—know exactly what works and are making small fortunes with it. The primary concept is that online marketing works best when you email to people who already know you. Therefore, successful online marketers build their house file or e-list (lists of prospects and their email addresses) using the process outlined below, and then sell to those people via email marketing.

1. Build a website that positions your newsletter, editor, or publishing company as an expert or guru in your field or topic. This is the base of operations for your online marketing campaign.

2. This website should include a home page, an 'About the Company' page, editors' biographies, and a page with a short description of each publication (each product or service overview can link to a longer document on the individual newsletter or advisory). Allow the visitor to read, print, and download a PDF of the most recent issue. Also post the current control promotion, typically your direct mail package converted into a long-form landing page linked to an order form.

3. You should have an 'Articles Page' where you post a few select articles taken from your newsletters that visitors can read and download for free. Don't give away your newsletters for free, of course. But give them a taste.

4. Write a short special report or whitepaper relating to a hot topic in your field, and make this available to people who visit your site. They can download it for free, but in exchange, they have to register and give you their email address and any other information you want to capture.

5. Consider also offering a daily, weekly, or monthly online newsletter, or e-zine. People who visit your site can subscribe free if they register and give you their email address. You may want to give the visitor the option of checking a box that reads, "I give you and other companies you select permission to send me email about products, services, news, and offers that may be of interest to me." A good example of a free e-zine is The Daily Reckoning (www.dailyreckoning.com) from Agora Publishing. Another is Morning Briefing from 21st Century Investor (21stcenturyinvestor.com).

6. The more free content (useful information) on your site, the better. More people will be attracted to your site, and they will spend more time on it. They will also tell others about your site. In time, your site will be regarded as the place to go online for information about your topic. The more people who visit for the free content, the more likely they are to read sample issues and sign up for your paid products.

7. The key, however, is to drive traffic to your site where you get them to sign up for either your free report or free e-zine. Once they register, you have their email address and can now market to them via email as often as you like. With this approach, you can market as many offers as you want, whenever you want, to your house e-list at virtually no cost. Therefore, even if the promotion pulls a very small response, it can still be immensely profitable. You can test

quickly and inexpensively, and read the results within forty-eight to seventy-two hours. How often should you email to your house file? Some publishers are having success with frequencies as high as two times a day. To test this, increase your frequency. When the opt-out rate suddenly increases, you know you have reached your maximum frequency.

Whenever someone clicks onto the landing page and order form for one of your paid products, but does not buy, they should get a pop-up screen as they click off. The pop-up invites them to sign up for a free report or e-zine on the same topic. This way, you capture their email address whether they buy or not.

8. The bulk of your online leads, sales, and profits will come from repeat email marketing to this house e-list of prospects. Therefore your goal is to build a large e-list of qualified prospects as quickly and inexpensively as you can.

9. There are a number of online marketing options that can drive traffic to your site. These include free publicity; email marketing; banner advertising; co-registrations; affiliate marketing; search engine optimization; direct mail; articles in other e-zines; cross-promotions with marketers reaching your audience; and e-zine advertising. Also be sure to capture the email addresses of readers who order by responding to your postal direct mail package. Do this by offering a free email alert or advisory as a bonus. To get the email advisory, the subscriber has to give you their email address.

10. The key to success in online subscription marketing is to try a lot of different tactics in small and inexpensive tests, throw out the ones that don't work, and do more of the ones that are effective.

CHAPTER 31

Creating Effective Websites for Subscription Products

What's working in websites for newsletter subscriptions and other information products? Here are twelve observations:

1. *Provide links to the order form early and often.* Marc Stockman of TheStreet.com says that placing links to order forms at the top of a landing page increases response. He also puts the call to action link throughout a landing page, not just at the end and the beginning.

2. *Use a dedicated microsite to sell directly off the webpage.* Yanik Silver, Fred Gleeck, Mark Joyner, Terry Dean, and other successful online information marketers, use dedicated microsites to sell e-books and other information products. Unlike traditional sites, with lots of free content and navigation capabilities and varied sections, microsites are basically a strong sales letter set up as a website. The only place the reader can click to is an order form for the product. For an example, see www.surefirecustomerservicetechniques.com, a microsite Mark Joyner did for my e-book on customer service.

3. *Personalization sells.* When you go to another Mark Joyner site, www.trashproofnewsreleases.com, this one on public relations, you are asked to enter your name. Then the website comes up with your name in the headline, "Joe Jones Will Be in the News in Forty-five Days or Less—Guaranteed," a clever and effective use of personalization.

4. *Establish credibility up front.* Yanik Silver, a successful online information marketer, observes that consumer skepticism online is even higher than offline. Therefore, you need to quickly build credibility. On Yanik's microsite www.instantsalesletters.com, he leads with three testimonials—and a link to dozens more—before he even gets to the first word of his headline.

5. *Offer a free e-zine.* The most profitable model in online subscription marketing is to build an e-list of subscribers to a free online electronic newsletter, or e-zine, and then promote to that list. The alternative—emailing to rented e-lists of opt-in names to acquire new subscribers—has met with extremely limited success. Your marketing website should have a prominent box for e-zine sign-up; see www.dailyreckoning.com again as an example. The Daily Reckoning is a free daily e-zine published by Agora, the financial newsletter publisher. They have hundreds of thousands of free e-zine subscribers to whom they market their paid subscription newsletters with great success.

If you have a microsite to generate orders for a single offer, you may not want to give potential buyers an alternative to purchasing your front-end product. Therefore, use a window for your free e-zine offer that pops up only after the buyer has either ordered your paid product or is clicking away from the microsite without ordering.

6. *Combine free and paid content.* An alternative to microsites are sites that combine both free and paid content. A good example, mentioned earlier, is TheStreet.com. Many of the articles are free; some are not. If you attempt to read an article that is not free, you are taken to a 'bridge page' (also known as a 'barrier page') that explains how you can read the article and others like it by subscribing to a paid service, such as TheStreet.com's *RealMoney*.

Another example is the home page of *The Bahamas Report,* www.thebahamasreport.com, a subscription newsletter about retiring in The Bahamas. There is a section 'Islands of the Bahamas' where, when you click on the name of a specific island, you get a free short report on that island. Below that is a section 'Recent Articles.' When you click on the article title you want, you are told you must subscribe to their online newsletter to read the article.

7. *Avoid sterile copy.* In the belief that online users don't read, have short attention spans, and do not like sales copy, many web marketers make their sites very plain and unexciting. "Make it look like information, not sales hype," some experts advise. But just because someone is online does not mean they don't have to be sold on your product. They do—as strongly as you sell them in print. Terry Dean, a successful online information marketer, packs his microsites with copy that reaches prospects on a personal and emotional level, not just intellectually. The lead sentence in a microsite selling membership to his subscription site Net Breakthroughs reads, "In just a moment, I hope to make you so angry you'll want to throw your computer right out the window."

8. *Offer a choice of monthly or annual subscriptions.* Subscription websites or newsletters promoted online should give the subscriber a choice of monthly or annual payments. Salon.com, for instance, allows you to subscribe monthly for six dollars or take an annual subscription for thirty dollars. The annual fee for online subscriptions is typically ten to twenty percent less than the monthly option. Salon.com is unusual in that their annual rate is less than half the equivalent cost of paying monthly for the subscription.

9. *Offer free trials and strong guarantees.* Guarantee satisfaction unconditionally. E-book marketers, for instance, offer a money-back guarantee even though the product, sent as a digital file, is not truly returnable—and they know the refund requestor is going to keep it. Another effective offer is the thirty-day free trial, where you take the credit card information online but tell the buyer you will not process it for thirty days—allowing them to try the product for

a month free. If they cancel within the thirty-day trial period, the card is never charged.

10. *Know your numbers.* A variety of services and programs are available for tracking website metrics. You can find a listing of some of these vendors at www.evendorsonline.com. The most important metrics are number of hits, conversion rates (percentage of hits who actually buy the product), and average size of order. From this, you can calculate the value of each hit. For instance, if your conversion rate is one percent and your product costs one hundred dollars, you will make one hundred dollars in revenues for every one hundred hits. If you are willing to break even to acquire a new customer, you can afford to pay up to one dollar per hit in marketing costs.

11. *Position your site as the premier online resource in your topic.* You can increase traffic and therefore revenues by positioning your site as a value-added information resource on your subject, not just a sales vehicle to push a paid subscription product. When you visit www.nanotechplanet.com, you are told you have reached "The Center for Nanotechnology Business." News briefs, articles, stock information, a glossary, FAQs, and other features reinforce that image and feeling.

12. *Push your primary offer like crazy.* At www.consumerinfo. com, the simply designed site has one goal: to get you to accept their offer of a free credit report. The home page is totally focused on this offer, as are two pop-up windows that come up when you log onto the site. When you click away, two more pop-up windows again make the same offer.

CHAPTER 32

Four Ways to Increase Your Direct Mail Response Rates When Selling Subscriptions

Despite declining response rates, direct mail is still the most profitable and effective method of generating subscriptions for newsletters. Four major factors affect the performance of your direct mail package:

1. The list.
2. The offer.
3. The format.
4. The copy

Traditional marketing advice says that the list and the offer are the most important factors, with copy and design (of which format is a subset) being far less critical. Well, yes and no. Here's what I mean. Yes, the list and offer are the most important factors affecting response rates, but you can identify, fairly quickly and easily, those lists that work best for your publication. If you publish a stock market newsletter, for instance, there is a limited universe of 'hard money' lists that all publishers know about and routinely test. They know that these are the only lists that usually work for stock market newsletter promotion, and this knowledge has already been gained through long experience; there is no need to reinvent it for each new financial newsletter.

For a particular publication, your initial test determines which of these lists are going to work for you. New lists come onto the market infrequently, so once you know what works, there's little additional leverage to be gained in the list area.

Next in importance is offer. But again, offers for newsletters—unlike some products, such as consulting services or software—are fairly simple, standard, and straightforward. Yes, there are variations. But your initial tests will quickly yield an offer that becomes the standard for your publication. After that, there's little additional leverage to be gained in the offer area.

That leaves us with copy and format. And even though these areas may affect response less than list and offer overall, once list and offer are set, the only additional leverage you can get is in testing new copy and formats. Therefore copy and format become of paramount, not secondary, importance, the only place where you can realistically hope to beat your control. Let's talk about copy first.

My rule of thumb in direct marketing is to observe what the largest direct marketers in your industry do, and copy them. Why? They mail many more pieces than you do. Therefore, they have more test experience. The greater the accumulated wisdom gained through testing, the more the marketer knows about what works and what does not work for their product. The largest newsletter publishers, such as Boardroom, Phillips, Agora and KCI do a lot of copy testing. They would not continue to mail large tests and pay top dollar to copywriters for direct mail packages unless they found the effort worthwhile and profitable. Therefore, it probably makes sense to do more copy testing than you currently do. At the very least, don't go out with just one package on a product launch or test. Create at least two versions, e.g., two different outer envelope teasers (or a teaser versus no teaser) and letter leads (headline and body copy on page one of the sales letter).

The most important part of the copy to test is the teaser, headline, or lead, and what you should be testing are two different 'big ideas' or concepts, e.g., "tastes great" versus "less filling." A winning headline or concept test can increase response rates twenty-five to one hundred percent, or even more—a much greater improvement than minor copy tweaks in the body of the package letter or brochure. For instance, the publisher of a newsletter on commodities trading tested two headlines: (a) "The Greatest Market Discovery Ever Made" and (b) "Only Two Commodity Markets Are Going to Return Explosive Profits This Year." In this test, (b) underperformed ( ) by twenty-five percent.

The second area where you have great leverage is in format. To begin with, test a letter package versus a self-mailer. If the letter package wins, think about testing a #10 versus a 6 x 9 envelope, versus a jumbo envelope. If the self-mailer wins, test a magalog versus a tabloid, versus a digest, versus a bookalog.   There is no standard format that remains the champion for all newsletters all the time. Different formats seem to perform best for different products at different times. A major publisher of health newsletters told me recently that for her company, nothing can beat a jumbo package. A large publisher of financial newsletters says that only magalogs are working for him now. But one of his competitors has five newsletters, and controls for all five are #10 packages. Go figure.

Even if the format does not change, varying the design alone can make a significant difference. Designer Ted Nicholas once beat a control package for a client by one hundred percent by changing only the design and not a word of the copy. And a major publisher of consumer newsletters tested two versions of its control, identical in every way except (a) had a white outer envelope and (b) had a kraft outer envelope. The kraft version (b) underperformed the white control version (a) by twenty-five percent.

So when an expert tells you, "Lists and offer are everything; copy, design, and format are unimportant," don't you believe it for a second.

CHAPTER 33

Best Direct Mail Package Formats for Marketing Business-to-Business Newsletters

Years ago, there wasn't much doubt about what direct mail format worked best for business-to-business newsletters: number ten outer envelope, four-page sales letter, one or more enclosures (sample issue, brochure, buck slip, lift note), four by nine-inch order card, and number nine business reply envelope.

But with rising postage and printing costs, and declining response rates, publishers are finding it harder and harder to make the traditional #10 direct mail package pay off for business-to-business newsletter offers. Many publishers are turning to shorter, smaller formats—from double postcards and tri-fold self-mailers, to vouchers and invitations. So I asked some of my colleagues—in both business and consumer newsletter publishing—what's working for them now.

"In general, #10 packages still work best," says Bill Dugan, Publisher, Briefings Publishing Group. "Sometimes the 9 x 12-inch flat envelope size works, too. Copy length is irrelevant. Direct mail copy needs to be as long as it needs to be to secure the sale. I don't believe there are any firm rules about copy length."

"Forced-free trials are still our number one promotion," says Jim Bell at IOMA, noting that approximately fifty-five percent of his sales come from telemarketing and forty-five percent from forced free trials. The company is testing some other traditional direct mail, but has no results to share yet. As for copy length, "like everything else, you have to test," says Bell. "The four-page letter that works on product X may not work on product Y."

"In my experience, #10 or 9 x 12 seems to work best to business audiences," says copywriter Don Hauptman. "I've rarely heard of magalogs or self-mailers working. Exception: sample issues with a wraparound can work well. "Over the years, I've seen an increasing trend: shorter copy beating longer copy to business audiences. Cutting eight pages to four, or four pages to two, can boost response. "The underlying principles, I think, are that people are busier at work than at home, and that you have to get past the gatekeeper and offer something of value."

And copywriter John Clausen comments, "I'm still finding that double postcards work well as part of a campaign. They're cheap and quick to produce and people are used to receiving them. Vouchers are good, too, for the same reasons. "One of the formats that I think is being overlooked is the jumbo double postcard. It has a lot of the advantages of a regular postcard but allows for more flashy design and more copy."

Steve Ackerman of American Health Consultants says, "Overall, forced free trials are still the best performing packages. And overall, short copy works best for us."

"We don't do any business-to-business stuff, but my guess is that business-to-business newsletters use #10 packages the most—lots of official-looking brown kraft and plain white envelopes," says Brian Kurtz of Boardroom. "On the copy front, since the lists are usually so targeted and vertical, I think you don't need more than four-page letters. But they have to get to the point fast because your audience is busy folks with isolated interests."

Increasingly, business-to-business publishers selling newsletters and journals at high price points—say $500 a year and up—are doing it through special sales: a direct sales force that calls on prospects in person or on the phone, and often sells them a group or site subscription instead of just an individual subscription. In such a case, your direct mail package isn't truly closing the sale. You aren't asking for payment or even a commitment to a paid subscription. At most, you are asking the subscriber to accept a no-risk free trial on a soft offer. Shorter formats seem to work well in these situations; Institutional Investor, for instance, uses voucher mailings to sell expensive newsletter services to financial professionals in this fashion.

Here are some other helpful guidelines in choosing direct mail formats to sell business-to-business newsletter subscriptions:

1. On a launch, be safe, and go with the old standard: a #10 package with an outer envelope, two or four-page sales letter.

2. If you are doing a test, it makes sense to try radically different formats. If your control is a #10 package and you suspect short copy can work for your product, try a voucher or double postcard.

3. To improve return on investment from your package, test a version where you remove one or two of the elements, such as a brochure or buck slip. Often it has no effect on response.

4. Sample issue mailings work especially well when the format of the newsletter itself is a selling point—for instance, it's laid out in a neat way that makes it easy to scan and read. Sample issue mailings also work well when you are selling multiple subscriptions to a buyer who intends to distribute copies to his staff.

5. Business-to-business newsletters aimed at small business, So-Ho, and self-employed audiences often do better with a four-page letter, while business-to-business newsletters aimed at executives seem to prefer a one or two-page letter. Exceptions? Of course.

CHAPTER 34

What to Do When Your Direct Mail Package Bombs

We've all been there. You put your heart and soul into writing the strongest direct mail package you know how to. You put it into the mail with high hopes and great expectations. And then zilch. Zero. Nada. Nothing. The package bombs. Big time. What do you do? What *can* you do? And, should you do it? Following are some guidelines for actions to take in the wake of a direct mail package that doesn't work nearly as well as you wanted it to.

1. In a launch, if the best package you could create doesn't come anywhere even close to break-even, it's probably the product, not the promotion. Simply put, the newsletter is a bad idea: The topic won't work with that audience. Should you try again? Probably not. As in the stock market, in newsletter publishing, it's usually best to cut your losses early. If an idea isn't working, find another that will. But don't throw away more good money on a bad idea.

2. Realistically assess the negative affects of time- and event-based depressions in mailing results. Yes, 9/11, a stock market crash, or a hurricane can lower your response rates—but all the way to *zero*? If competitors are still doing a decent level of business despite the setback, and your response is nil, then you can't blame the economy, the environment, or the market. There's a deeper flaw in your mailing which sending it out again at a better time will not likely rectify.

3. Study your list results. If just one or two lists pulled a halfway decent response—even though, overall, the mailing was unprofitable—there may be a glimmer of hope. You may want to retest the winning lists along with additional lists that reach a similar audience. I cannot overemphasize the need to test as many lists as possible. Even for business-to-business newsletters reaching narrow vertical markets, the best-performing list may out-pull the worst performing list by five to one or more though, on the surface, the lists and the market they reach appear almost identical. You simply have to test.

4. Perhaps there are markets that are not price sensitive, but most are. Have you tested enough price points to find whether what you're asking is what the customer is willing to pay? Keep in mind that the low price doesn't always win. A price that is too low can create the perception of low value, an impediment to brisk sales.

5. Many of us think the market for our information is much larger than it really is. As a result, we often dilute our direct mail copy by spending too much time appealing to secondary markets. While the layperson may think a dentist is a dentist, the truth of the matter is that a D.D.S. is likely to have widely different information needs than an endodontist, periodontist, or orthodontist. The narrower and more precisely you define your target market, the easier it becomes to write direct mail copy that is meaningful, relevant, and appealing.

6. Lack of market focus is one reason for unprofitable newsletter subscription promotions. Lack of topic focus for the newsletter itself is another. Professional speaker, Wally Bock, defines a niche as the intersection of a topic (customer service, sales, marketing, pricing, stress management, computer skills) with an audience (accountants, lawyers, doctors, plumbers, architects). If your audience is, say, accountants, focus on teaching them or keeping them up to

date on what you know best. If that's client retention, don't dilute your newsletter and promotions with ancillary topics, such as time management, succession planning, or tax law. Stick to client retention.

7. What if direct mail for a once-successful newsletter is not pulling well any more? Should you tweak the package, or come up with and test an entirely new mailing? There are several schools of thought. Many practitioners routinely vary just the front end of their direct mail packages—the outer envelope teaser, letter headline, and the first page of the copy. If successful, this kind of front end testing—which is really the testing of new package concepts or ideas—can increase results twenty-five to fifty percent, and in some cases even one hundred percent. "You don't have to spend a ton of dough on new creative," writes copywriter Doug D'Anna in *Hotline* (October 15, 2002, p. 3). "Take your tired, worn-out old control and add new life by simply writing two or three new test headlines and letter leads."

8. Another school of thought follows the Japanese model of continual improvement or *kaizan*, the idea being that many small, incremental improvements can add up to an overall large improvement. These direct marketers constantly test new testimonials, new premiums, new offers, new terms, and new guarantees. They vary outer envelope stock and color, periodically update body copy to freshen it up, and replace older bullets with newer examples. They also add and subtract package elements such as lift notes, buck slips, premium sheets, tokens, stickers, and other inserts and involvement devices. While this can work, it's slow going, and my experience is that a front end test as outlined by Doug D'Anna (rewriting the teaser and letter lead) is the quickest and lowest cost way to significantly improve results.

9. Copywriter Gary Bencivenga says that a format test—varying the package size and type—can be as effective, or even more effec-

tive, than a copy change in lifting response. If you already know that short copy works best for your publication, test your #10 letter package against a double postcard, voucher, snap pack, invitation, wrap, forced free trial, and other proven short formats. If you already know that long copy works best for you, test your #10 letter package against a #11 or a #14, a 6 x 9, a jumbo (9 x 12). Also test against a magalog, a digest, a tabloid, and a bookalog.

10. Testing leads, format, and copy tweaks can all work, but don't forget the most basic approach used by virtually every major publisher of consumer health care and financial newsletters: testing brand-new creative packages. One problem with headline and lead testing is that the package, as mailed, doesn't integrate the new idea or theme expressed in the headline throughout the rest of the copy because it's just a new headline pasted on old copy.

Creating a fresh, entirely new package helps ensure that the new idea is communicated consistently and powerfully in every sentence. The disadvantage of creating a lot of new test packages is the cost. Many copywriters will give you a new headline and lead test for a fraction of what they charge for a completely new package. A solution might be to negotiate the cost of doing new headline and lead tests at the time you contract with the copywriter to do a fresh package. That way, if you want to test new heads and leads after the initial package has mailed, the fee is already established and you can budget for it in advance. Expect to pay from fifteen percent to fifty percent of the original package fee for a separate headline and lead test, depending on the magnitude and scope of the changes required to implement the new creative idea.

CHAPTER 35

Which is Better to Enclose in Your Direct Mail Package— a Sample Issue or a Brochure?

When creating a direct mail package selling a newsletter subscription, you know you're going to have an outer envelope, a sales letter, an order form, and a business reply envelope. But what else? Should you use a sample issue or specimen issue? Or is a sales brochure better? Here are the options available and guidelines for selecting the right one for your package and your product.

1. *Sample issue*. Use a sample issue when there is something inherently appealing about the format of the newsletter itself. One example is *Communication Briefings*, whose presentation of bite-size tidbits of information can only be communicated effectively with a sample issue. Likewise, the major advantage of *Bits & Pieces*—*the* fact that it fits easily in a shirt pocket—is best demonstrated with a sample.

2. *Specimen issue*. A specimen issue is a sample issue that is not the actual newsletter from any particular month, but rather a sample composite assembled from articles taken from multiple monthly issues. You can use an actual issue as your sample if you have an issue with broad, strong, almost universal appeal to the entire base of potential subscribers. Avoid using actual issues whose main cover story or theme is of interest only to a limited portion of the potential subscriber base; in such cases, a specimen is preferable.

3. *Full-size brochure.* The full-size brochure is an 11 x 17-inch sheet folded to form four pages. Use a full-size brochure when you want to reprint sample pages from the newsletter large enough to be readable. Call-outs can indicate the unique editorial features contained on each page. A full-size brochure is also useful for illustrating multimedia products such as, a loose-leaf service with various multiple components like the binder, tabs, supplements, special inserts, and a CD-ROM.

4. *Slim Jim brochure.* A slim Jim brochure is typically an 8 ½ x 11-inch sheet of paper folded twice to form six panels. You can also use an 8½ x 14-inch sheet folded three times to form eight panels. Use the slim Jim when there is a limited amount to say or illustrate beyond what is already included in your sales letter.

5. *Premium sheet.* A premium sheet is typically an 8½ x 11-inch sheet of paper printed on one or both sides. It is used to highlight premiums and their contents, although other information, such as an editor's biography, may also be included. Premium sheets are used when there are multiple premiums (usually three or more) that need to be pictured and described in some detail.

6. *Buck slip.* A buck slip is typically a 4 x 9-inch sheet of paper printed on one side. Buck slips are used to highlight premiums. They work best when you have only a few premiums (three or fewer) that need minimal copy to describe.

7. *Lift letter.* The lift letter is a second letter inserted with the package, usually Monarch size. It can be used either to reinforce a point made in the main sales letter, or introduce an additional selling point or supporting sales information not included elsewhere in the package.

CHAPTER 36

Selling Subscriptions
With Forced Free Trials

With response rates to traditional number ten packages and other direct mail formats in decline, newsletter publishers are once again turning to a proven marketing method that periodically comes in and out of favor: forced free trials.

In a recent survey, the Newsletter and Electronic Publishers Association (NEPA) asked its members (all newsletter publishers) which marketing channel brings in the most orders. The number one newsletter subscription marketing method was direct mail, cited by 50.9 percent of those surveyed. Forced free trials came in second, with 20 percent of the vote. Telemarketing was a close third, at 18.2 percent.

In his book, *Success in Newsletter Publishing: A Practical Guide* (Newsletter Publishers Association), Frederick Goss defines a forced free trial as a promotion in which "a selected number of prospects are given a trial without their having requested it." It is "forced" because the recipient is going to get the issues whether he wants them or not! The idea is that by 'forcing' samples of your publication upon the recipient, you will convince those for whom the publication is a good fit that it is worth their while to read and subscribe to. They are willing to receive and read the issues because the trial subscription is free and they need not take any action to request it. Therefore sales resistance to receiving their free issues is at a minimum.

In comparison, a direct mail promotion which requires the reader to mail back a card to request free issues generates significant sales resistance, and only a small percentage of recipients will agree to receive the free issues, even if there is no commitment and no money required up front.

The primary advantage of a forced-free trial is it allows the potential subscriber to sample the publication without making a purchase or taking action of any kind. There are at least three other ways to sell newsletter subscriptions through sampling:

1. Mail a free sample issue with a wrap to a list of prospects.

2. Enclose a free sample issue in your direct mail package.

3. Offer a free sample issue to anyone who responds to your package.

The three options above, however, only allow the prospect to see one sample issue. If the articles in the sample issue do not match the prospect's interests, he may decide against subscribing.

The advantage of a forced-free trial is that the prospect gets to read multiple issues of the publication. Therefore, the chances of his seeing articles relevant to his interests are much higher than with single-free-issue promotions. Goss describes one newsletter publisher's typical forced-free trial program as consisting of six mailings and five issues on a biweekly (basis). The issues go with mailings one through five, the reply form and business reply envelope (BRE) with mailings one, four, five, and six.

Jean Jennings, a well-known consultant in the newsletter industry, suggests the following sequence of mailings for a forced-free trial promotion:

1. Initial contact: first issue with a welcome letter.

2. Week #2: second free issue.

3. Week #4: third free issue with first invoice.

4. Week #6: fourth free issue.

5. Week #8: fifth free issue with second invoice.

6. Week #10: third invoice (no issue).

The above schedule, which calls for five free issues, is for a twice-monthly publication. For a monthly publication, Jennings suggests sending three free issues.

Efforts can vary, but the typical package components in a series of forced-free trial mailing are the issue, a one-page cover letter, an invoice or reply form, and a business reply envelope. Always include language on the invoice or reply form that says, "This is not bill and you are under no obligation to pay." Trying to fool the recipient into thinking they ordered the publication and have to pay your invoice is deceptive.

The first mailing in a forced-free trial program almost always contains an issue and a letter explaining to the reader that he has been selected to receive a free trial of the publication. Typically the rationale is that the reader is someone important or active in the industry, and therefore the content of the publication is of vital interest. The letter enclosed with the first issue should explain to the reader how to opt out or cancel the trial subscription. After all, if someone is certain they do not want the publication, giving them a way to opt out saves you the cost of sending five more mailings to a person who is never going to buy.

In her book *The Ultimate Guide to Newsletter Publishing* (Newsletter and Electronic Publishers Association), Patty Wysocki recommends putting a teaser on the outer envelope that reads, "Here's your free trial issue," which gets the word 'Free' on the outer envelope. I prefer the teaser "Your current issue enclosed" because it gives the impression that you are delivering a publication to which the reader already subscribes, which, in a sense, is true since they have not cancelled the free trial subscription you are giving them. A corporate mail room is less likely to throw the envelope away if they think it contains a publication the reader has paid for.

The main disadvantage of forced-free trials is cost. You are sending six mailings (a combination of sample issues, letters, and order forms) instead of a single direct mail package. For this reason, forced-free trials are used almost exclusively with business-to-business newsletters costing a minimum of two-hundred dollars a year, or more. You almost never see forced-free trials used with lower-priced consumer newsletters.

As response rates to traditional direct mail promotions—long the staple of newsletter subscription marketing—continue to struggle, newsletter publishers are looking for other channels of distribution. Some are beginning to have success with telemarketing, although the national Do Not Call list may have a negative effect on the telephone as a subscription marketing medium, however, publishers finally understand how to effectively use the Internet as a subscription marketing medium.

Forced-free trials are staging a comeback. Should you test them? Yes, if you publish a business-to-business newsletter with a high price point and targeted at a well-defined target market for which quality mailing lists are available.

CHAPTER 37

Blanket Renewals

Advance renewals, also called *blanket renewals*, often generate the highest response rates and profits of any direct mail piece a newsletter publisher can mail, yet many publishers don't use them effectively or at all. They are called 'advance' because the goal is to renew the subscriber early, before the regular renewal cycle begins. However, 'blanket' is a more accurate term, since these renewals are sent to all subscribers at the same time, regardless of where that individual subscriber is in the life of the subscription. Therefore, some of the renewals may not be reaching all subscribers in advance of the regular renewal letter series. Some may arrive during that series.

Those who do not use blanket renewals object to the idea as follows: "Why send these extra renewal efforts at all that extra expense? They will just get us renewals we would have gotten later down the road with our regular renewal series." My answer is that those future renewals orders are a 'maybe.' Maybe you will get the numbers your renewal plan projects; maybe you won't. But every renewal order that comes in through a blanket renewal is money in the bank now, not later.

An advance renewal is sent either as a separate mailing in an envelope or enclosed as an insert with the subscriber's regular issue. When you are sending your blanket renewal as a stand-alone package, make the word 'renewal' prominent on the outer envelope, the first page of the letter, and the order form. 'Renewal' gets the attention of existing subscribers. Blanket renewals sent as solo mailings are similar in style, tone, length, and format to regular renewal efforts and consist of an outer envelope, a one or two-page letter, a reply form, and a business reply envelope. Sometimes there is a lift note or, to highlight a premium, a buck slip.

Blanket renewals designed as inserts typically range from four pages in length and occasionally eight pages. Depending on how you mail your newsletter, some of the pages of the renewal insert may have to be dedicated to pure editorial to satisfy postal requirements. When in doubt, ask your postmaster.

What themes can you effectively build your blanket renewal efforts around? Here are six techniques proven to work for a variety of different newsletter publishers.

1. *Avoid future price increases.* When there is no other news or angle, you can make the primary reason to renew now instead of later the ability to lock in the current price and avoid future price increases. This can work all the time, since publication prices go up frequently and almost never get cheaper. So it is believable. When you can give a concrete reason why the newsletter price may go up soon, this approach is even more effective.

2. *Sell the offer.* When you have a special blanket renewal offer, stress the offer, not the publication. The more attractive the offer, the more it should be highlighted in the promo. Offers that work best include:

(1) Discount for early renewal.

(2) Extended subscription for early renewal (two extra issues).

(3) Special premium for early renewal.

(4) Value-added service free with early renewal (telephone hotline or website access).

Does that mean you don't talk about the newsletter at all, and focus only on the offer? No. You *do* need to resell the newsletter, and that's a good tactic to take in the lead when there is no special offer. But if you have an enticing *offer,* lead with that first.

3. *Correct the defects.* Savvy publishing companies adjust their product and offer based on subscriber feedback. A blanket renewal is an excellent forum for talking about those fixes. After all, you are asking the reader to continue subscribing. He is more likely to do that if you have corrected the defects in your product that were bothering him. For instance, a subscriber survey for an investment letter showed that readers were unhappy with the lack of mutual fund coverage. To correct the defect, the editor produced a special videotape in which he discussed mutual funds. The videotape became the premium for a very successful advance renewal mailing.

4. *Explain the discount with unconventional reasoning.* KCI Communications has had great success with *Utility Forecast* advance renewals that feature arguments between the editor and publisher (Roger Conrad and Walter Pearce) where they 'fight' over the price (and the editor, who wants to hold prices down, wins). For example, when *Utility Forecaster* increased its page count from eight to twelve pages per issue (increasing the length fifty percent), they sent a blanket renewal insert with this headline, attributed as a quote to the editor. It worked extremely well:

> "Making these improvements to *Utility Forecaster* raised my publisher's cost 50% per issue, but I told them YOU shouldn't pay even a nickel more!"

5. *Look for and exploit a 'twist'* One investment letter did a reader survey that showed subscribers made surprisingly few and infrequent trades. A successful advance renewal took the subscriber to task for not taking advantage of opportunities—and offered extra issues for early renewal to provide readers with a chance to get in on stocks they may have missed earlier:

"If you missed out on making 186%, 410%, or even 725% on these winning recommendations from *Personal Finance*, I'll extend your subscription for FREE while there's still time to get in on these top profit-making recommendations."

6. *Be straightforward—but quirky.* Make the offer clear and sell it hard, but add a story or other element of intrigue to boost reader interest. Example: *Growth Stock Winners* offered as a renewal premium a bonus report listing of stocks of greater than usual profit potential and risk—so aggressive that the publisher would not 'allow' the editor to present them in regular issues!

CHAPTER 38

Nine Ways to Sell High-Priced Information Products

When selling specialized information products such as newsletters, journals, conferences, online services, loose-leaf services, home study courses, videos, audio albums, or multimedia programs, we are often asking prices that are many multiples of what trade publishers charge for books and magazines. The higher the price, the more the prospect is likely to experience sticker shock—a resistance to paying that much money for information, no matter how much he wants it. Fortunately, there are a number of promotional techniques that can help us overcome sticker shock and get people to pay the hefty prices we are asking for our print or online information services.

1. *Make the reader relieved to hear how little you are charging.* Do this by stating higher prices for other services or products first, then giving your price, which is less. For instance, if you are selling reading specs, mention that laser eye surgery is over a thousand dollars and new eyeglasses can run three hundred dollars at an optician's, but your buy-by-mail reading specs are just $19.95.

If you are selling an options trading course on video, first mention your one million dollar minimum private managed accounts and your five thousand dollar seminars. By the time you get to the videos, the prospect will actually be relieved that they are only $299.

2. *Make an apples-to-oranges comparison.* Don't compare your newsletter to another newsletter. Compare it to another information resource, such as private consultation or expensive training. Promotions for Georgetown's *American Speaker*, a loose-leaf service, compare the $297 price to the $5,000 a top speechwriter would charge to write just one speech. A promotion for *Leeb's Index Options* Alert noted that the $2,950 it charges for its options trading fax service is like paying a 2.95 percent fee on a $100,000 managed options account—and that it's actually lower than the total fee such a managed account would charge.

3. *Spread out the payments.* Rodale and Franklin Mint are well aware of the sales-closing benefits of offering several smaller payments vs. one large lump sum. One financial publisher sells online trading advisories costing thousands of dollars. They found that offering subscriptions on a quarterly basis reduced sticker shock and increased sales. If yours is an Internet service, consider offering it for so much a month with credit card payment on a 'till forbid' basis. After all, which sounds better—"$19.95 a month" or "$240 for one year of service?"

4. *State the price in terms that make it seem smallest.* Even if you want full payment up front, state the price in your promotion in terms that make it seem smaller. A $197 annual subscription, for instance, gives the buyer access to vital information for just 54 cents a day. Warning: Divide the price by length of service or subscription, but *avoid* a price per book or price per page comparison. Reason: Specialized information products always have a higher price per page than the trade books or periodicals with which the buyer will invariably make a comparison.

5. *Value the component parts.* If you are selling an options trading course for two hundred dollars, list the individual elements and show that the retail prices of each (videos, workbook, telephone hotline, website access) add up to much more than two hundred dol-

lars—therefore the course buyer is getting a great deal. Even better: position one or two of the product elements as premiums the buyer can keep even if he returns the product or cancels the subscription. Offering 'keeper' premiums usually increases response. Example: instead of selling your eight-cassette audio album for sixty-nine dollars, say it is a six-cassette album for sixty-nine dollars and then position the other two cassettes as premiums.

6. *Add an element that cannot easily be priced by the buyer.* Looseleaf services, for instance, face a built-in resistance from the buyer: "Why is it $199 dollars if it's just a book?" Supplements help differentiate from regular books, but publishers have found it even more effective to include a CD-ROM with the notebook. The CD-ROM is perceived as a high-value item with indeterminate retail price (software on CD-ROM can cost anywhere from $19 to $499), so it destroys the 'book to book' comparison between loose-leafs and ordinary books.

7. *Show the value or return on investment in comparison to the price.* Demonstrate that the fee you charge is a drop in the bucket compared to the value your product adds or the returns it generates. For instance, if your service helps buyers pass regulatory audits, talk about the cost of failing such an audit—fines, penalties, even facilities shutdowns. If your manual on energy efficiency in buildings cuts heating and cooling costs ten to twenty percent a year, the reader with a $10,000 fuel bill for his commercial facility will save $1,000 to $2,000 this year and every year—more than justifying the $99 you are asking for the book.

8. *Find a solution with your pocket calculator.* With intelligent manipulation, you can almost always make the numbers come out in support of your selling proposition. Example: a high-priced trading advisory specializes in aggressive trades with profits of around twenty to thirty percent with average holding periods of less than a month. The challenge: overcome resistance to paying a big price

for modest-sounding returns. The solution: dramatize the profits the subscriber can make with numerous quick trades. Copy reminds readers: "If you could earn five percent each month for the next ten years, a mere $10,000 investment would compound to a whopping $3.4 million. At ten percent, it would be an almost unimaginable $912 million!"

9. *Pre-empt the price objection.* Most mailings for expensive products build desire and perceived value, then reveal price once the customer is sold. An opposite approach is to state price up front and use the exclusivity of a big number to weed out non-prospects. Example: "This service is for serious investors only. It costs $2,500 a year. If that price scares you, this is not for you." An element of exclusivity and snob appeal is at work here. Also, the more you tell someone they do not qualify, the more they will insist they do and want your offer.

The classic example is Hank Burnett's famous letter for the Admiral Byrd Society's fund-raising expedition. The second paragraph of the Burnett letter states: "It will cost you $10,000 and about twenty-six days of your time. Frankly, you will endure some discomfort, and may even face some danger."

10. *Do a false close.* Bring the prospect to the point of asking for the order, then instead of doing so, say "But wait, there's more" and then present another irresistible benefit. *Then* ask for the order.

11. *Add a sweetener.* Add an extra incentive—a special premium, extended warranty or guarantee, free service or support, two for the price of one, or other special offer to close the deal.

12. *Establish the editor or publisher as the leading expert in your field.* Price resistance diminishes in direct proportion to the prospect's belief that you are the unchallenged expert in your field or niche. Reason: they perceive you offer solutions unavailable from other sources, and that your solutions work as promised. PR works

well here: readers will pay more for your publication if the editor has a TV show. My book, *Become a Recognized Authority in Your Field — in 60 Days or Less* (Alpha Books), is packed with strategies on how to establish your reputation as a leading guru.

CHAPTER 39

Eight Ways to Enhance Credibility When Marketing Newsletters

"People buy from people they like and trust" is an established sales truism, but how many people receiving your direct mail package have even heard of your publication or editor or you, much less like and trust you? Your direct mail copy must work hard to build the credibility that will get the reader to trust you enough to order and rely on your information. Here are some techniques copywriters use to establish credibility quickly in their mailings.

1. Show a picture of your building or establish a physical presence to prove you're more than just a mailbox. Promotions for *Dr. Atkins' Health Revelations* show a photograph of his impressive seven-story clinic in midtown Manhattan and note that tens of thousands of patients have been treated there.

2. Link the specifics of the editor's background to reasons why this particular background enhances his value as a researcher and analyst. A promotion for *Forecasts & Strategies* notes that editor Mark Skousen was once with the CIA, which gave him government insider contacts he still uses today to interpret the market for his readers. Likewise, promotions for *Technology Investing* point out that Michael Murphy's proximity to Silicon Valley enhances his ability to research high-tech companies first-hand.

3. Cite any awards the publication has won or favorable third-party reviews it has garnered. These can include Newsletter and Electronic Publishers Association awards and, for financial newsletters, favorable ratings in *The Hulbert Financial Digest*. (Since some readers may not be familiar with the source of the rating, describe it in impressive terms—Hulbert, for instance, can be described as "The *Consumer Reports*" of the financial newsletter industry.)

4. Get and use testimonials from subscribers and the media. The best testimonials are specific rather than superlative, and support the key points you are making in your copy.

5. Stress the editors' credentials and experience. List the books they have written (and their publishers) and the periodicals in which their articles have appeared. Also list major conferences and speaking engagements as well as academic or business affiliations. Give the names of the TV and radio shows or stations that have featured the editors as guests.

6. If the editors are not subject matter experts and the publication is not built around them, promote the credibility of the publisher instead. Tell how many publications you have and why you have such a great reputation in the market you serve.

7. One way to get around an editor or publisher credibility problem is to create an editorial advisory board. Have three to five experts agree to be on this board then stress their credentials and achievements in your promotional copy.

8. Don't forget standard credibility stuff, like number of years in business or number of subscribers—especially if you have been in business a long time or have an unusually high number of subscribers. "Our 50th year" impresses some people. Also look for other statistics that can boost your credibility. For example, perhaps you still have your first subscriber who joined twenty-eight years ago when you published your first issue.

Part V

Business-to-Business and High-Tech Marketing

CHAPTER 40

Ten Ways to Increase Response Rates to Direct Mail Selling Software

Are you planning to test a new direct mail package to promote your software? Following these ten, simple steps can help you avoid common mistakes, increase response, and tip the odds of having a profitable mailing in your favor.

1. *Product.* What are you selling? A stand-alone PC application? An enterprise-wide system, such as supply chain management (SCM) or customer relationship management (CRM)? A Web application that must be integrated with back-end systems? Study the promotions from successful software companies in your category. Do you sell tax or accounting software? Reply to an Intuit mailing and see what happens. Selling databases? Check out what Oracle is doing.

Analyze the structure, format, and content not only of the initial direct mail piece, but also of the entire marketing campaign, from generating the inquiry to closing the sale. Chances are companies with products similar to yours, especially the successful ones, have developed these marketing models through expensive trial and error testing. Why not copy what works and avoid the cost of going down the wrong path? Things to look out for when modeling your efforts after the marketing campaigns of successful software publishers include offer, pricing, media, formats, the mix of online and offline marketing methods, lead qualification, the discrete steps that take a potential buyer from an inquirer to a closed sale, and number and types of communications used in each.

2. *Offer.* What offer would work best for your software? For low-priced products costing under five hundred dollars, the mail order model—selling the software directly from the direct mail package—is possible and should be tested. If it works, that is, if the package generates sales that are one and a half times or more of its total cost in the mail (printing, letter shop, postage, and lists), then you have a winner.

If the product is enterprise software or other applications selling for $5,000 or more, you will probably need to use a two-step, or lead-generating, direct mail model. The direct mail piece generates an inquiry, which is then fulfilled and followed up by mail, phone, Web, in person, or some combination of these. The sale is closed in the follow-up, not in the initial mailing. One thing that works with a $5,000 product is to offer a "Small Project Version" or other smaller version for a nominal fee, say $50 or $99. The small version has all of the features of the full product, but is limited in some way—for instance, the "Small Project Version" of a project management program may only allow up to ten tasks in a project plan. If the customer decides to buy the full version, the money he paid for the small version is credited toward the purchase of the complete program. If the price of your software is between $500 and $5,000, you are in a gray area. You have to experiment to see whether you should go for sales or leads.

When generating leads, offering a premium usually increases response. "Whitepapers on websites, informative online newsletters, even thinly disguised bribes are used to prompt dialog," says copywriter George Duncan. Other premiums that have worked well for software marketers include print whitepapers, CD-ROMs, software utilities on diskette, ROI calculators, checklists, and 'needs assessments'—such as forms that can be used to evaluate whether there is a need for the software, or how to plan for its installation and deployment.

3. *Price.* Direct mail is a medium that works well when special offers, such as discounts, are used. Do you want to get $300 for your software? In the mailing, say that it is regularly $399 (yes, supermarket pricing works below $1,000), but if they buy now it is only $299. A $100 savings is a proven offer for mail-order software marketing.

For more expensive software, state the license price per user. "Just $50 per user for 100 desktops" sounds more affordable than "$5,000 for up to 100 users." Software with a high price often causes "sticker shock." To offset this, show a strong return on investment. Example: a direct mail package for surfCONTROL, a program that monitors employees' Internet access, says that if an employee wastes an hour a day in non-work-related Web surfing, and their time is worth $60 an hour, the cost in lost productivity is $300 a week—$15,000 per employee per year. The copy then compares the elimination of that lost productivity with the $2 per user licensing fee.

4. *Audience.* Analyze the audience: their needs, interests, problems, concerns, awareness of the problem your software solves, level of PC literacy and sophistication. "With end-to-end productivity solutions, you have two audiences—executive management and information technology," notes Duncan. Executive management wants to know the business benefit: lower costs, increased productivity, improved customer service, higher profits. Information technology wants to know whether the software is compatible and easily integrated with their existing systems.

A helpful exercise is to analyze what is known as the buyer's "core complex," abbreviated BFD for beliefs, feelings, and desires. These are the emotions, attitudes, and aspirations that drive your prospect:

(1) *Beliefs*. What does your audience believe? What is their attitude toward your product and the problems or issues it addresses?

(2) *Feelings*. How do they feel? Are they confident and brash? Nervous and fearful? What do they feel about the major issues in their lives, businesses, or industries?

(3) *Desires*. What do they want? What are their goals? What change do they want in their lives that your product can help them achieve?

For instance, we did this exercise with IT people, for a company that gives seminars in communication and interpersonal skills for IT professionals. Here's what we came up with in a group meeting:

(1) *Beliefs*. IT people think they are smarter than other people, technology is the most important thing in the world, users are stupid, and management doesn't appreciate them enough.

(2) *Feelings*. IT people often have an adversarial relationship with management and users, both of whom they service. They feel others dislike them, look down upon them, and do not understand what they do.

(3) *Desires*. IT people want to be appreciated and recognized. They also prefer to deal with computers and avoid people whenever possible. And they want bigger budgets.

Based on this analysis, particularly the feelings, the company created a direct mail letter that was its most successful ever to promote its seminar, "Interpersonal Skills for IT Professionals." The rather unusual headline mentioned earlier was, "Important news for any IT professional who has ever felt like telling an end user, 'Go to hell.'" Before writing copy, write out in narrative form the BFD of your target market. Share these with your team and come to an agreement on them. Then write copy based on the agreed BFD.

5. *Medium.* The choice of medium depends on the available list, offer, the product, and the audience. Is your audience very Internet-oriented (e.g., web masters)? Ask your list broker for recommendations on e-lists. Using email instead of paper direct mail might make sense, especially if you can direct them to a strong website that can drive the sale or the download of a demo or evaluation copy.

If you have a specialized audience numbering in the thousands or tens of thousand (CPAs, dentists), direct mail can work well if a list is available targeting this specialized group of users. For a product with broad appeal and a potential market in the hundreds of thousands or millions (e.g., software to prepare a will or make greeting cards), newspaper ads can work well. On the other hand, if you have a narrow audience of only a few hundred potential buyers, such as software for robot manufacturers, telemarketing may be the way to go.

6. *Format.* Say direct mail is the medium of choice. What format will work best for you? "When you want to drive prospects to a website where an uncomplicated transaction can take place, oversized postcards are frequently effective," says Duncan. For generating inquiries for a PC program, the traditional direct mail package—outer envelope, sales letter, brochure, order form, and business reply envelope—is the format of choice.

What about high-end solutions, like CRM, SCM, and ERP (enterprise resource planning)? "Because of the costs involved, and the fact that these purchases are made by committee after an exhaustive review process, prospects are difficult to reach and engage," says Duncan. "Three-dimensional mailings are often effective for this purpose, but can result in unqualified responses. Given the price points involved, however, such responses are far more acceptable than they used to be."

7. *Lists.* Contact one or two list brokers and ask for list recommendations. These are presented in *data cards*—sales sheets de-

scribing the number and type of people on the mailing list. Always go to an experienced list broker for list recommendations. Do not call the list owner directly. If you call the list owner (e.g., a computer magazine), they will want to rent you their list, whether it's the best for your offer or not. A list broker, by comparison, is not promoting a specific list. Their advice is more objective. Their interest is in getting you the lists that will work best for you, so you will come to rely on their list recommendations and rent more lists from them. Many software marketers do not realize that the recommendations of a list broker involve no charges; they earn a commission on the cost to rent the lists. You pay the list broker only when you rent names from the lists they find for you. They do not mark up the lists. The list owner pays their commission. That means you pay the exact same price as if you rented the list directly from its owner.

The mailing list is the most important element in direct mail, affecting response rates up to one thousand percent, or more! And with more than thirty thousand lists available, only a professional list broker has the time to keep up to date on what's available and what will work for your business.

8. *The USP.* With so many software products on the market today, how do you make yours stand out? You must define its unique selling proposition (USP). This is the reason why the customer should buy your program instead of your competitors. Many marketers have heard of USP, but very few remember the three characteristics of a successful USP, first defined by Rosser Reeves in his 1961 book *Reality in Advertising* (Alfred A. Knopf):

(1) Each advertisement must make a proposition to the consumer. Each advertisement must say to the reader, "Buy this product, and you will get this specific benefit."

(2) The proposition must be one that the competition either cannot or does not offer. It must be unique—either a unique-

ness of brand or a claim not otherwise made in that particular field.

(3) The proposition must be so strong that it can move the mass millions, i.e., pull over new customers to your product. (In the case of software, this may be the mass thousands rather than millions, but the idea is the same.)

Why is having a USP so important? Think about it: if you don't know what sets your product apart from the competition, or why people should buy your program instead of theirs, how do you expect to convince complete strangers to do so?

9. *The Big Promise.* Samuel Johnson said, "Promise, large promise, is the soul of an advertisement." Once you have defined a USP, convert it into a big promise—a succinct, compelling statement of why the prospect should buy your product. The big promise can usually be stated in fifteen or fewer words, and used as the headline of an ad or the outer envelope teaser of a direct mail package. For instance, "Develop Clipper applications four times faster—or your money back," for an application development tool.

The headline is the most important part of any promotion, so once you have written it, try to make it even better and stronger. One useful technique for this is the "Four U's." Ask yourself whether the headline is urgent, unique, ultra-specific, and useful (i.e., promises a benefit). A software marketer wrote to tell me he had sent out an email marketing campaign with the subject line "Free Whitepaper." How does this stack up against the Four U's?

(1) *Urgent.* There is no urgency or sense of timeliness. On a scale of one to four, with four being the highest rating, "Free Whitepaper" is a one.

(2) *Unique.* Not every software marketer offers a free white paper, but many do. So "Free Whitepaper" rates only a two in terms of uniqueness.

(3) *Ultra-specific.* Could the marketer have been less specific than "Free Whitepaper"? Yes, he could have just said, "free bonus gift." So we rate "Free Whitepaper" a two instead of a one.

(4) *Useful.* I suppose the reader is smart enough to figure the whitepaper contains some helpful information he can use. On the other hand, the usefulness is in the specific information contained in the paper, which isn't even hinted at in the headline. And does the recipient, who already has too much to read, really need yet another "Free Whitepaper"? I rate it a two. Specifying the topic would help, e.g., "Free Whitepaper shows how to cut training costs up to ninety percent with e-learning."

Rate your Big Promise headline in all Four U's on a scale of one to four (one is weak; four is strong). Then rewrite it so you can upgrade your rating on at least two and preferably three or four of the categories by at least one point on the scale. This simple exercise may increase readership and response rates substantially for very little effort.

10. *Content.* Content refers to the rest of the copy. How much copy should there be? What information should it present? At what level of technical detail and in what order? Should you give features, benefits, specifications, data, test results, testimonials, or all of them?

A key issue is the information density of the copy. For most software products, you can literally write a book about the product (proof of this is the thousands of computer books published each year). But in direct mail, you don't have that space, so you have to be selective. If telling everything about the product would sell it, we'd simply mail prospects the book.

A useful exercise in planning the content and organization of your mailing is to divide a sheet of paper or Word file into two columns. Label the left column 'features' and write down your product's features. In the right column, write down the corresponding benefit, and label this column 'benefits.' Now put the list of features and benefits in order of importance. The first feature/benefit should be the one that corresponds with the big promise. This becomes the lead of the package—the outer envelope teaser, letter headline, and letter lead.

The next three to six feature/benefit combinations are the most important after the big promise, and are highlighted in the sales letter. They may also be amplified upon in the brochure.

The rest of the features/benefits are secondary and can be covered in the brochure. A table works well for features and benefits. Specifications can be put in a separate box or sidebar.

A useful rule of thumb when determining content and information density is to include only what it takes to get the prospect to take the next step in the buying process. If it's to go to a URL and download a free demo, that probably requires a lot less information than getting the prospect to order a $299 PC application sight unseen.

CHAPTER 41

Should Business-to-Business Copy be Shorter than Consumer Copy?

"What's the most effective length for a business-to-business sales letter?" a reader asked me the other day. Let me see if I can give some sensible guidelines to answer this common question.

To begin with, most of my colleagues in direct marketing agree that the trend in copy length is this: consumer mailings are getting longer, while business-to-business mailings are getting shorter. Consumer mailings are getting longer because prospects are more skeptical than ever, hence they need more sales arguments to convince them to buy. Business mailings are getting shorter because business prospects are increasingly pressed for time. Some consumers are too, but not all.

We can divide business-to-business letters into two categories: lead-generating letters (designed to generate an inquiry) and mail-order letters (designed to generate an order). As a rule of thumb, lead-generating business-to-business letters are either one or two pages in length, while mail-order business-to-business letters are typically two to four pages in length. Lead-generating business-to-business letters can be short because they do not have to do the whole selling job like mail-order copy must. In a lead-generating letter, you only have to whet the prospects' appetites; that is, get them to take the next step in the buying process. Typically, that step is either requesting more information, such as a sales brochure or catalog, or meeting with a sales representative. The sales representative, brochures, and catalogs give the product details. All the letter has to do is to convince the prospects to raise their hands and express interest in learning more about the product or service.

Whether the letter is one or two pages is very important. A one-page letter works best with extremely busy readers, such as business executives and doctors, who don't have the time or inclination to read long copy. When they open the envelope and see that the letter is only one page, they relax enough to quickly scan it and learn whether they want to reply or not. To this group, a multi-page letter gives a visual clue that the package is a lot to read, which is an immediate turn-off and a signal to trash it or put it aside.

You can comfortably go to two pages when writing to audiences who are either (a) readers, (b) possibly not quite as busy and pressed for time as executives and doctors, e.g., middle managers, entrepreneurs, farmers, engineers, and IT professionals, or (c) have a strong, personal interest in the proposition of the letter (selling a small business owner software to run his company, as an example). A two-page letter gives you a bit more room to include points that can help convince the reader to respond, e.g., testimonials, product features, and other details. There is also more room to appeal to a breadth of emotions, feelings, beliefs, or copy points. For a non-personalized letter, the two-page letter can be printed on the front and back of a single sheet of 8½ by 11-inch paper. If the letter is personalized, use two separate sheets of paper.

But what if two pages isn't enough room to fit in all your sales arguments? One solution is to include a slim-Jim brochure in the mailing. A slim-Jim is a letter-size or legal-size piece of paper folded two or three times vertically to form a brochure that fits into a #10 envelope. The old saying in direct mail is "the letter sells, the brochure tells." The letter presents the main selling arguments; the brochure contains supporting evidence including product photos, diagrams, graphs, specifications, features, background on the company, testimonials, a customer list, and so on. Instead of a slim-Jim brochure, I sometimes prefer to enclose with my letter a reprint of an article about the company or the product. Reason: the article looks more like useful information vs. a brochure which looks like advertising matter. If no articles written about or by your company exist, you can design an insert to look like one.

Now let's leave lead-generating letters and discuss mail-order letters—letters designed to bring back an order. In mail-order selling, there is no brochure the reader can send for to get the detailed product specs and features, and no sales rep to answer questions. The mail-order letter must do the whole selling job alone, and for this reason, longer copy is needed. Consumer mail-order sales letters are often four to eight pages or longer. The business-to-business mail-order letter can range from one to eight pages in length, but most often, they are either two or four pages.

You should never mail a three-page letter; a blank page is a waste of space. If the letter layout comes to three pages, either condense it to two pages using a tighter layout and smaller type, or expand it to four pages using a looser layout and larger type. I prefer the latter; large type and roomy layouts are more inviting and easier to read. In all cases, the letter should be only as long as it needs to be to get the selling job done and maximize the response. Therefore a letter for a complex product with many features and benefits, such as software, will typically be longer than a letter for a simple product or service, such as a janitorial or office cleaning service.

The prospect's level of interest and involvement with the product is another key factor determining letter length. IT managers will be highly interested and involved with the selection of a major new software system; after all, technology is their main interest. So they will read a relatively large amount of copy about the product.

On the other hand, dentists hiring office-cleaning services only care that the offices are cleaned reliably and at a reasonable price. Dentists are not as interested in the details of office cleaning as they are in the details of a new teeth-whitening system. Therefore, they will not have great interest in reading about the cleaning service and its methods in detail. But they probably will read long copy about "how to build a million dollar dental practice" because it is so much more interesting and relevant to their goals, dreams, and desires.

CHAPTER 42

Other Differences between Business-to-Business and Business-to-Consumer Marketing

After a quarter-century in business-to-business marketing, I think I've finally figured out an accurate, authoritative answer to the question, "What's the difference between business-to-business marketing and business-to-consumer marketing?" The answer, in my opinion, is this: the business buyers need your product—the actual, physical product, not just its benefits—and wants to spend his money on it. Yes, the benefits are critical, but they need more than just the benefits or advantages; they also need the actual product itself—a fax machine, personal computer, domain name, credit line, or pollution control system. The consumers want the benefits your product delivers, but do not want the product itself. Nor do they want to part with their money to obtain it.

Let's compare two different products, a business product and a consumer product. The consumer product is a monthly financial newsletter that tells individual investors what stocks to buy. The business product is a valve used in the chemical process industry.

In the case of the valve, your customer, an engineer—let's call him Pete—is not merely looking for a set of benefits (e.g., the ability to control fluid flow). Pete is looking specifically for a valve. His processing plant uses many valves, and when one has failed or the plant is being expanded, he needs another valve. Nothing else will do. Pete wants to buy a valve—the physical product—and he knows what he wants. He most likely does not have to be sold on the idea of using valves; he already uses them. (Yes, there may be exceptions, such as when another piece of equipment could be used in place of a valve.)

Pete *does* have to be sold on whether to buy your valve vs. another brand or model. Although Pete may have a budget that constrains his selection of valve manufacturer and model, he is not opposed to the idea of spending money on valves. He does not resist it. As a plant engineer, spending money on valves is actually part of Pete's job description: to not buy valves would be paramount to a dereliction of duty—the duty to keep the plant operating reliably and efficiently. So Pete wants to buy, and he wants to spend his company's money to acquire this product.

Now let's take Pete's father, Tom, also an engineer but now retired. Tom spends a good part of his retirement, as do many white-collar men who have been successful, managing his stock portfolio and other investments. (I am not being sexist by saying "men"; the majority of subscribers to investment newsletters are men over 60 years old.) Tom has several things he wants. One is to make money with his stocks. Another is not to lose the gains he makes. So he desires profit and safety. Tom does not need a stock market newsletter. Thousands of Americans trade stocks every day having never subscribed to a financial advisory. Remember, as Bill Bonner of Agora Publishing is fond of saying, "Nobody wakes up, shakes the other person sleeping in the bed, and says, 'Honey, we need to get more newsletters today!'" What Tom is after is the benefit of the product—increased stock market profits with greater safety. He does not need the product. But more than that, he does not *want* the product itself—eight to twelve pages of paper with ink on them—either. The fact that the product is a newsletter may very well be a negative to Tom. He may feel he already has too much information to read, and no time for yet another publication. He wants the benefit, but not the physical product itself.

Unlike Pete, who is mandated to spend his company's money on valves as part of his job, Tom would rather not part with his money to get the benefits (greater portfolio returns) he seeks if he can help it. In fact, there are many other information providers offering financial advice in print and online at much lower cost than your newsletter, and a good number of them don't charge at all. If Tom believed that free information would help him meet his investment objectives as well as your stock market newsletter, he'd take that free information and happily avoid ordering your newsletter.

But Tom is suspicious of free advice; he believes you get what you pay for. He also believes that many of the sources providing him with free investment advice—stockbrokers, for example—are not objective and have self-serving motivations. Because you charge for your advice and are supposedly unbiased (your consumer newsletter carries no advertising), Tom is willing to pay one hundred dollars to receive your publication—even though he would prefer not to spend the money or have another newsletter to read. Amazing, isn't it?

Part VI
Copywriting

CHAPTER 43

Thirty-eight Ideas for Your Next Headline

The best way to get ideas for headlines when you are stuck is to keep a swipe file of successful headlines, and consult it for inspiration when you sit down to write a new ad or mailing. As a shortcut, here's a partial collection of such headlines from my vast swipe file, organized by category so as to make clear the approach being used.

1. *Ask a question in the headline:* "What Do Japanese Managers Have That American Managers Sometimes Lack?"

2. *Tie-in to current events:* "Stay One Step Ahead of the Stock Market Just Like Martha Stewart—But Without Her Legal Liability!"

3. *Create a new terminology:* "New 'Polarized Oil' Magnetically Adheres to Wear Parts in Machine Tools, Making Them Last Up to 6 Times Longer."

4. *Give news using the words "new," "introduction," or "announcing:"*
"Announcing a Painless Cut in Defense Spending."

5. *Give the readers a command—tell them to do something:* "Try Burning This Coupon."

6. *Use numbers and statistics:* "Who Ever Heard of 17,000 Blooms from a Single Plant?"

7. *Promise the reader useful information:* "How to Avoid the Biggest Mistake You Can Make in Building or Buying a Home."

8. *Highlight your offer:* "You Can Now Subscribe to the Best New Books—Just as You Do to a Magazine."

9. *Tell a story:* "They Laughed When I Sat Down at the Piano . . . But When I Started to Play."

10. *Make a recommendation:* "The Five Tech Stocks You Must Own NOW."

11. *State a benefit:* "Managing UNIX Data Centers—Once Difficult, Now Easy."

12. *Make a comparison:* "How to Solve Your Emissions Problems—at Half the Energy Cost of Conventional Venturi Scrubbers."

13. *Use words that help the reader visualize:* "Why Some Foods 'Explode' In Your Stomach."

14. *Use a testimonial:* "After Over Half a Million Miles in the Air Using AVBLEND, We've Had No Premature Camshaft Failures."

15. *Offer a free special report, catalog, or booklet:* "New Free Special Report Reveals Little-Known Strategy Millionaires Use to Keep Wealth in Their Hands—and Out of Uncle Sam's."

16. *State the selling proposition directly and plainly:* "Surgical Tables Rebuilt—Free Loaners Available."

17. *Arouse reader curiosity:* "The One Internet Stock You MUST Own Now. Hint: It's NOT What You Think!"

18. *Promise to reveal a secret:* "Unlock Wall Street's Secret Logic."

19. *Be specific:* "At Sixty Miles an Hour, the Loudest Noise in This New Rolls Royce Comes from the Electric Clock."

20. *Target a particular type of reader:* "We're Looking for People to Write Children's Books."

21. *Add a time element:* "Instant Incorporation While U-Wait."

22. *Stress cost savings, discounts, or value:* "Now You Can Get $2,177 Worth of Expensive Stock Market Newsletters for the Incredibly Low Price of Just $69!"

23. *Give the reader good news:* "You're Never Too Old to Hear Better."

24. *Offer an alternative to other products and services:* "No Time for Yale—Take College At Home."

25. *Issue a challenge:* "Will Your Scalp Stand the Fingernail Test?"

26. *Stress your guarantee:* "Develop Software Applications Up to Six Times Faster or Your Money Back."

27. *State the price:* "Link Eight PCs to Your Mainframe—Only $2,395."

28. *Set up a seeming contradiction:* "Profit from 'Insider Trading'—100 Percent Legal!"

29. *Offer an exclusive the reader can't get elsewhere:* "Earn 500+ Percent Gains With Little-Known 'Trader's Secret Weapon.'"

30. *Address the reader's concern:* "Why Most Small Businesses Fail—and What You Can Do About It.'

31. *As Crazy as It Sounds:* "Crazy as it Sounds, Shares of This Tiny R&D Company, Selling for $2 Today, Could be Worth as Much as $100 in the Not-Too-Distant Future."

32. *Make a big promise:* "Slice Twenty Years Off Your Age!"

33. *Show return on investment for purchase of your product:* "Hiring the Wrong Person Costs You Three Times Their Annual Salary."

34. *Use a "reasons-why" headline:* "Seven Reasons Why Production Houses Nationwide Prefer Unilux Strobe Lighting When Shooting Important TV Commercials."

35. *Answer important questions about your product or service:* "Seven Questions to Ask Before You Hire a Collection Agency … and One Good Answer to Each."

36. *Stress the value of your premiums:* "Yours Free—Order Now and Receive $280 in Free Gifts With Your Paid Subscription."

37. *Help the reader achieve a goal:* "Now You Can Create a Breakthrough Marketing Plan Within the Next 30 Days—for FREE!"

38. *Make a seemingly contradictory statement or promise:* "Cool Any Room in Your House Fast—Without Air Conditioning!"

CHAPTER 44

What Works Best:
Long Copy or Short Copy?

Since time immemorial—or at least for the quarter-century I've been in direct marketing—people have vigorously debated the merits of long versus short copy. "If you are selling something worth more than twenty dollars, I'll put my money on longer copy every time, because it gives me a chance to provide more facts, benefits, and credible copy," says Jim Murphy. "And I'll put my money on a direct mail kit over a self-mailer because, with a kit, I have a chance to get your order with the letter, brochure, or order form."

I don't pretend that I can settle the debate once and for all. But I've developed a tool, which I call the Copy Length Grid (see Figure 1), that can at least enable us to determine copy length in a somewhat more scientific and semi-quantitative fashion. The Copy Length Grid says there are two major factors determining whether long or short copy will work best for your promotion: emotion and involvement.

Emotion refers to the degree to which the purchase is emotional. Buying a diamond engagement ring is a highly emotional purchase, while you are moved very little emotionally when deciding which brand of paper clips to buy.

Involvement refers to how much time, effort, and thought goes into the product purchase. As with most large purchases, a lot of consideration goes into the selection and purchase of a diamond engagement ring. But most of us grab the first box of paper clips on the shelf of the stationery store without giving it a second thought.

To use this system for determining copy length, rate these two criteria—emotion and involvement—as high or low. This dictates what quadrant of the Copy Length Grid you end up in, which in turn gives you at least a rough guideline for copy length. For instance, the purchase of a diamond engagement ring is highly emotional. And, it's a 'considered purchase'—something you give a lot of thought to—so it rates high in involvement. As you can see in Figure 1, this puts us firmly in the upper left quadrant of the grid, indicating that long copy is appropriate for this offer.

On the other hand, paper clips are more of an impulse purchase; when we need them, we go to the store and pick up the first box we see, providing it's the right size. There's no emotion and very little thought that goes into this purchase. This puts us in the lower right quadrant of Figure 1, which indicates that writing long, passionate copy about paper clips probably isn't going to sell more of them.

Of course, the Copy Length Grid is only a rough guide, not a precise analyzer. There are a number of other factors that also must be taken into account when determining copy length. These factors include:

1. *Price*. The more expensive a product, the more copy you generally need to sell it. Lots of copy is needed to build the case for value before asking for the order, so that when the price is finally given it seems like a drop in the bucket compared to what the buyer is getting in return.

2. *Purpose*. Copy that sells the product directly off the printed page or screen (known as *one-step* or *mail-order* copy) usually has to be long, because it must present all product information and overcome all objections. Copy designed to generate a lead (*two-*

step copy) can be short, since a catalog, brochure, or salesperson will have the opportunity to present product details and overcome objections later.

3. *Audience.* People who are pressed for time, such as busy executives and professionals, often respond better to short copy. Prospects with more time on their hands, such as retirees, as well as those with a keen interest in your offer, such as hobbyists, are more likely to read long copy.

4. *Importance.* Products that people *need* (e.g., a refrigerator, a bed) can be sold with short copy because the prospect *has* to buy them. Products that people *want* but don't *have* to buy (e.g., exercise videos, self-help audio programs, financial newsletters) must be 'sold' and require long copy to do so.

5. *Familiarity.* Short copy works well with products the prospect already is familiar with and understand. This is why vouchers and double postcards are used so frequently to sell subscriptions to popular, well-known magazines (e.g., *Newsweek, BusinessWeek*).

Based on the Copy Length Grid and these other factors, clearly long copy is not always better, and there are many instances when short or almost no copy works well. This is the case with items that sell themselves, such as staplers or garden hoses. But for items that have to be intensively sold—life insurance policies, luxury automobiles, IT systems, collectibles, high-end jewelry, career training—long copy is often required because of the degree of emotion and involvement.

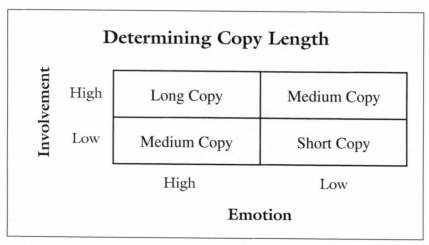

Figure 44-1. The Copy Length Grid

CHAPTER 45

The Awful Truth about High-Falutin' Copy

I frequently have to deal with this complaint, as it comes up fairly often and, recently, I heard it from a new client who wanted to sell web services to marketing managers at Fortune 500 and middle market corporations. "This copy is too simple," the client said. "This sounds as if you are talking to small business owners. Our audience is senior managers at Fortune 500 companies. The tone needs to be much more professional and sophisticated." Oh, really? Says who?

One of the biggest misconceptions about writing to CEOs, CFOs, and other senior executives is that they speak some alien language that has only a passing resemblance to the conversational or written English you and I use every day, and—in order to sell to this special audience—you have to emulate or copy this special language. But the reality is that high-level executives read the same newspapers you do, go to the same movies, listen to the same radio stations, and watch the same TV shows. Yes, it's smart marketing to understand your audience and then write copy that speaks to their specific needs, fears, concerns, problems, and desires. And you want to tailor the tone and style of your language to fit your audience to a reasonable degree. For instance, you wouldn't use off-color language when writing to ministers. Or use equations in differential calculus when writing to factory workers. But ministers, chemists, accountants, engineers, computer programmers, while they all may speak the specialized language of their trade, also speak a common language: the English language. And that's the language you should use when writing your copy.

How do I know I am right? The same way we know anything about direct marketing: through testing. I have tested plain English copy against high-falutin' copy numerous times over the span of my quarter-century career in direct marketing, and ninety-nine times out of one hundred, the same language that works for ordinary folks sells just as effectively to CEOs, Ph.D.s, and yes, even rocket scientists.

It is easy enough to see this for yourself. Study the controls in any market, for any kind of product. Collect as many direct marketing packages as you can that you know to be strong controls, because they have been mailed repeatedly. Now divide them into two piles: those written in plain English versus those written in jargon, big words, or high falutin' language. If you have collected a dozen samples, I guarantee that the number in the plain English pile will be twelve or eleven—no fewer than that—proving my point.

I recently interviewed more than a hundred CEOs, including those at many Fortune 500 companies, to ghostwrite a book titled, *Leadership Secrets of the World's Most Successful CEOs* (Dearborn). Without exception, they were all plain-speaking men and women, using direct, straightforward, conversational language in their written and oral communication. The world's most respected writing authorities all agree that good writing is clear, simple, and direct. "Clutter is the disease of American writing," writes William Zinsser in *On Writing Well* (HarperCollins, 2001, page 7). "We are a society strangling in unnecessary words, circular constructions, pompous frills, and meaningless jargon."

And what about my claim that good writing is conversational? "You can't actually write the way you talk," writes Rudolph Flesch in *The Art of Readable Writing* (Harper & Row, 1949, page 82).

"You can, however, put a reasonable facsimile of your ordinary talking self on paper. You can purposely put into your writing certain things that will make it sound like talk." (He cites contractions as one example.)

One other point: I have been writing copy aimed at engineers, scientists, mathematicians, systems analysts, and other 'techies' for twenty-five years. And in all that time, I've never once been told that the simple, plain English copy I wrote was too easy to read. Of course, you can always test my claim that plain English out-pulls high falutin' language for yourself. The next time a marketing manager says of your conversational copy, "It's not professional enough," offer to do a split test: your version against the marketing manager's version. Then you'll know definitely what works best for the target audience rather than relying on the marketing manager's opinion, your opinion, or my opinion. Make sense? Of course. Doing an *A/B* split test always does, right?

CHAPTER 46

How to Write Powerful
Bullets and Fascinations

One of the standard and most effective techniques for writing subscription copy is to present the publication's content as a list of bulleted items, e.g., "Seven ways to reduce your heating bill this winter." Many copywriters rattle off the bullets quickly and as a result settle for bullets that are rather ordinary, and therefore, not terribly engaging. It takes a bit more energy and creativity to come up with a bullet that is as strong and compelling as this classic from Boardroom: "What never to eat on an airplane."

Boardroom and other marketers call these bullets *fascinations*, so-named because the content they present or promise is fascinating to the reader—or at least, should be. For example, a promotion from Health Resources promoting a nutritional supplement contains bolded copy that reads, "Little-known secret could bring you real relief from joint problems." There are two key elements to fascinations demonstrated here. The first is the promise of a benefit: "relief from joint problems." The second element that makes it effective is that the solution or answer is promised, but not revealed. You have to order the product to find out how to relieve joint problems; all you are told is that it is a "little-known secret."

One of the common mistakes with bullets is not including the right level of information. "Tell too much, and you give away the information free, and there is no need to subscribe to the publication to find the answer," says copywriter Parris Lampropolous. "For example, if your bullet says 'how to erase pain by using an over-the-counter lotion called capsaicin,' no curiosity is generated because you've already told the secret." On the other hand, says Parris, if your bullet contains too little information, or not enough specific information, it fails to grab attention. "If you say 'why B vitamins are an absolute must for people predisposed to this disease,' you fail to hook me, because I don't know what 'this disease' is," says Parris. His rule of thumb for writing strong bullets: be specific about the *problem*; be vague and mysterious about the solution.

Plus, do it with a twist, hook, or unusual angle. He gives as an example a copywriter who had to write a bullet based on the fact that keeping your wallet in your back pocket can cause back pain because you are sitting on a bulky object. The bullet that the copywriter came up with: "How a pickpocket can make your back pain better." He is specific about the problem (back pain) but mysterious about the solution (how can a pickpocket help with back pain?).

CHAPTER 47

Persuasion Secrets of the Top Marketing Pros

For reasons I won't go into here, because they are boring and not germane, I planned to write a book years ago with the pompous title of *The Persuasion Manifesto*. I envisioned it as a massive compendium of persuasion techniques, expressed in practical how-to rules, as understood by top salespeople, copywriters, psychologists, and other masters of the psychology of influence. I immediately send an email to some of these folks requesting them to contribute a tip or idea for the book. Ten of them responded, and their replies are explored here:

1. *The 'so what' test.* After you write your copy, read it and ask whether it passes the 'so what' test. Copywriter Joan Damico explains: "If after reviewing your copy, you think the target audience would just respond with 'so what,' then keep rewriting until they'll say something like, 'That's exactly what I'm looking for. How do I get it?'" Copywriter's agent Kevin Finn adds: "When copy is being critiqued, you should ask after each and every sentence, 'So what?' It's a technique that can assist in changing copy to be more powerful."

2. *Use the key copy drivers.* Make sure your copy hits one of the key copy drivers as defined by Bob Hacker and Axel Andersson: fear, greed, guilt, exclusivity, anger, salvation, or flattery. "If your

copy is not dripping with one or more of these, tear it up and start over," says Denny Hatch.

3. *The 'drop in the bucket' technique.* "You have to show that the price you are asking for your product is a drop in the bucket compared to the value it delivers," says copywriter Mike Pavlish. Fred Gleeck says this is a function of product quality, not just copywriting. "Produce a product that you could charge ten times as much for," says Gleeck. "If you really have a product that is so much more valuable than the price you're charging, it becomes much easier to sell it hard."

4. *Know your audience.* Understand your target market—their fears, needs, concerns, beliefs, attitudes, desires. "My way to be persuasive is to get in touch with the target group by inviting one or two to dinner for in-depth conversation," says Christian Boucke, a copywriter for Rentrop Verlag in Germany. "I also call fifteen to forty by phone to get a multitude of testimonials and facts, and go to meetings or exhibitions where I can find them to get a first impression of their typical characteristics. Ideally, I accompany some of them in their private lives for years. By this, I understand better their true underlying key motivations."

5. *Write like people talk.* Use a conversational, natural style. "Write like you talk," says Barnaby Kalan of Reliance Direct Marketing. "Speak in language that's simple and easy to understand. Write the way your prospects talk."

6. *Be timely.* "Pay very close attention to goings-on in the news that you can and should link to," suggests Dan Kennedy in his *No B.S. Marketing E-Letter* (June 2002). "Jump on a timely topic and link to it in useful communication with present clients, in advertising for new clients, and in seeking media publicity."

7. *Lead with your strongest point.* "When I review my writing, or especially others, I find they almost always leave the most potent

point to the last line," says John Shoemaker. "So I simply move it to the first line. Instant improvement."

8. *The Tremendous Whack Theory.* "I employ Winston Churchill's 'tremendous whack' theory, which says that if you have an important point to make, don't try to be subtle or clever," says Richard Perry. "Use a pile driver. Hit the point once. Then come back and hit it again. Then hit it a third time—a tremendous whack."

9. *Build credibility with your reader.* "In my experience, the number one key to persuasion is this: communicate trust," says copywriter Steve Slaunwhite. "If you do this well, you at least have a chance at engaging and persuading the reader. If you don't do this well, however, no amount of fancy copywriting techniques will save you."

11. *Don't use an 'obvious lead.'* "Instead of writing your lead as if you are just starting to talk to the customer," says Bryan Honesty, "write as if you were already engaged in a conversation with the customer—and are just responding to her last statement." Examples: "You have the gift. You just don't know it yet." "You can't quit on your dreams now." "So why is it so hard for you to lose weight?"

CHAPTER 48

The Awful Truth Behind Search Engine Optimization Copywriting

Search engine optimization (SEO) copywriting requires that the copywriter concern himself with strategic placement of key words, tags, and the like within his web copy to optimize search engine rankings of the pages being written. The problem is that to create really powerful copy, you have to have a single core audience in mind and concentrate all your effort on writing to that one audience. When I write copy, that audience is the prospect, the potential buyer of the product I am selling. But with SEO copywriting, you are pandering to another audience—the search engines—and not the reader. And by creating copy that's optimal for attracting search engines, you are, to some degree, weakening that copy's power to sell. You dilute its strength, because you are worrying about two audiences—the reader and the search engines—instead of focusing every word squarely on the customer. And that's not how to write copy that sells. Here, in my opinion, is a much better approach to writing web copy.

1. Write the strongest selling copy you can aimed at the human reader and forget the search engines.

2. Once that copy is finished, go back and check to make sure key words are appropriately placed, but....

3. Never change a word of strong selling copy if that change

will make it even one iota weaker . . . even if SEO best practices would endorse that change.

4. Once the page is up and working (i.e., generating strong conversion), then you can optimize for search engines by experimenting with word changes—testing to make sure those edits don't reduce conversions.

In other words, write for the customer and not search engine optimization. A small informal survey I conducted shows that top copywriters—writers with proven track records of really making the cash register ring—agree. "I'd rather invest my time and energy in proven factors I can control, such as a potent headline and interesting, informative, and fact-filled copy," says copywriting legend Gary Bencivenga (www.BencivengaBullets.com). "Write your sites using the exact words that match the extremely narrow and specific way people search for information online. Nobody searches for 'automotive accessories.' Way too broad. They search for 'leather steering wheel covers' or 'fuzzy device. Much SEO advice comes from people who peddle it for a living," he adds. "I've heard that search engines modify their methodology regularly, to thwart those who try to 'fix the race.' So I view SEO as a mechanical rabbit I'll never be able to catch."

And when I asked copywriting great Parris Lampropoulos whether he concerned himself with search engines when writing web copy, his answer was, "Not at all. When I'm writing the copy, I'm working at one task and one task only: to get whoever is reading it to place the order," says Parris. "Later on, after the copy is up and pulling orders, the client may test changes to see if they can increase SEO without hurting response."

"I agree in principle. You should always write for your audience—in this case, the people who visit your web page via search engines," says direct marketing consultant Bob McCarthy. "But let's be practical. If you don't appease the search engines, you don't have an audience. If optimizing your web pages for search engine marketing is going to multiply your visits by let's say ten times, wouldn't some copy trade-off be worth it?"

Dianna Huff, a recognized expert in business-to-business marketing communications writing, with extensive knowledge of SEO, takes pains when writing copy to optimize each page's search engine ranking. "As a marketing writer—one who is trying to get a prospect to take action—I write to that audience," says Dianna. "But I also write with the search engines in mind. It takes just as much talent and strong writing to write meta titles and descriptions that people will click on in the search engines. There is no point in writing good copy on your site if no one can find you. According to a survey by Enquiro and MarketingSherpa on the role of search in the business-to-business buying process, over sixty percent stated they research products online anywhere from two to twelve months out in advance of a purchase, and sixty-nine percent choose the organic listings first. If your company isn't listed due to poor SEO, then you're not getting that click. And then, if someone gets to your site and it is lacking in content, as many business-to-business sites are because they are just brochure-ware, then you've just lost a valuable lead."

"Most of the good SEO things you can do have to do with page structure and linking relationships among pages, not the copy," says Don Marti. "Getting incoming links from reputable pages is much more important than having copy that is somehow 'search engine friendly' on its own."

John Ford, a top copywriter for Agora Publishing, says he doesn't give any extra thought to search engines when writing on-line promotions, in this quote:

> "It's certainly true that you can kick your ranking up in the Google search by focusing on the right keywords and looking at lists of keyword usage. It's amazing, actually,

how easily this can be done. And shocking, I think, that some people get paid quite a bit of money to do only this.

I've got two thoughts on SEO copywriting. First, one has to question the business model. I have yet to see anyone show that high rankings in the search engines directly correlate to greater sales. The major successes online, that I've seen anyway, have all been from people who have found some other way to actively drive known prospects and repeat customers to their online sales promotions. This might mean e-newsletter-driven sales, print advertising or inserts, well-placed endorsements, or editorial mentions. But, not to any great degree, the randomness of a search engine search. This is not to say there's NO money to be made with SEO marketing, just that there are much more lucrative ways to increase your response rates.

Second, a lot of what counts for success in SEO marketing seems so obviously connected to just hitting the right 'hot buttons' for your prospect in the first place. A good direct response copywriter writes very specific and, usually, benefit-oriented headlines and leads. This means using words you believe your prospect is most likely to respond to when he or she reads them.

What's the secret to good SEO copywriting? Figuring out the specific, benefit-related keywords your prospect is most likely to type into a search engine. That is, the words he or she most likely connects to your product. What's the difference between that and standard copywriting? Not all that much in my estimation.

Want to be a great SEO copywriter?

Then just be a great copywriter period. When you're done writing, match your lead against an online list of the highest related keywords, and maybe you'll end up tweaking a word or two. But that's it.

Of course, I'm sure you have your own opinion on SEO and copywriting. So, what say you? Do you put the reader—or he search engine—first? Is there a conflict between writing to attract search engines and writing for people? Or are the two activities complementary?"

CHAPTER 49

Selling with *False Logic*

False logic, a term coined by my friend, master copywriter Michael Masterson, is copy that manipulates (but does not lie about or misrepresent), through skillful writing, existing facts. The objective is to help readers come to conclusions that those facts, presented without the twists of the copywriter's pen, might not otherwise support. A catalog for Harry & David says of its pears, "Not one person in one thousand has ever tasted them." The statistic, as presented by the catalog writer, makes the product sound rare and exclusive—and that's how the average reader interprets it, just as the copywriter intended. But a logician analyzing that statement might say that it simply indicates that the pears are not very popular—almost no one buys them.

It's possible to argue that some false logic borders on deception, but the marketer has to make that call for himself. A metals broker advertised, "Ninety-five percent of orders shipped from stock" to indicate ready availability. But he ran his business out of an office and had no warehouse. How could he claim he shipped from stock? "We do ship ninety-five percent of orders from stock," the marketer explains. "But not from *our* stock—from the *metal supplier's stock*. We are just a broker. But we do not advertise that, since being a broker is perceived as a negative."

A promotion selling a stock market newsletter to consumers

compares the $99 subscription price with the $2,000 the editor would charge if he were managing your money for you, based on a two-percent fee and a minimum investment of $100,000. The readers think they are getting Mr. Editor to give them $2,000 worth of money management services for $99, and quickly gloss over the fact that the newsletter is not precisely the same as a managed account.

A similar example is the promotion done by my friend Don Hauptman for *American Speaker*, a loose-leaf service for executives on how to give good speeches. In his promotion, he points out that this product can help you with your speeches all year long (it has periodic supplements) versus the $5,000 it costs to have a professional speechwriter write just one speech. But of course, American Speaker is not actually writing your speech for you.

There is an ongoing debate of whether people buy for emotional or logical reasons, but most successful marketers know that the former is more dominant as a buying motive than the latter. It is commonly said, "People buy based on emotion, then rationalize the purchase decision with logic." Because they have made the buying decision based on strong feelings and ingrained beliefs, they are in essence looking for justification and support for what they already want to do. Therefore, as long as the logical argument seems credible and sensible, they will accept it. They do not probe into it as scientifically or deeply as would, say, Ralph Nader or an investigative reporter for *Consumer Reports*.

Some critics view direct marketing as a step below general marketing in respectability, ethics, and honesty. And perhaps they might reason that my advocating the use of false logic adds fuel to their argument. But in fact, false logic is not just the purview of direct marketers; general marketers use it routinely, some with great success. For years, McDonald's advertised, "billions sold" to promote their hamburger—leading customers to the false conclusion that just because something is popular, it is necessarily good. Publishers use similar logic when they trumpet a book as, "a *New York Times* best-seller."

Is all this unethical? You can draw your own conclusion, but in my opinion, no. A copywriter, like a lawyer, is an advocate for the client (or his employer). Just as the lawyer uses all the arguments at his disposal to win the case, so does the copywriter use all the facts at his disposal to win the consumer over to the product. We should market no products that are illegal, dangerous, or immoral, though one man's *Victoria Secrets* catalog is another man's soft porn. But, to not use all the tools at our disposal (including false logic) to persuade the buyer is either incompetence, failure to discharge fiduciary duties, or both.

CHAPTER 50

Roster Reeves' Three-part Formula for Creating a Winning *Unique Selling Proposition*

Here's a trick question: What's better: chopped liver or filet mignon? Most people answer filet mignon. But filet mignon isn't better than chopped liver. Nor is chopped liver better than filet mignon. Here's the mistake most people make: if you picked filet mignon, you should have said, "I like filet mignon better" and not, "filet mignon *is* better." One is not inherently superior to the other. It's a matter of taste. You like filet mignon, so to you, filet mignon is better. But I like chopped liver, so to me, it's not.

So what does this have to do with your business? Plenty. Every business needs to have a unique selling proposition, or USP, a reason why customers should buy from you instead of from your competitors. Do you know what the weakest unique selling proposition is? It's "we're better." Better, you see, is nonspecific, and it's difficult to prove. You say you're better. I say I'm better. It's difficult to prove, and just *saying* it causes prospects to disbelieve you. Also, better is such a general term, that it has little meaning. Same thing with the overused, 'quality.'

So how do you create a unique selling proposition that actually gets people to want to buy your product instead of the competition? There are many methods, but let me describe just three of them here.

The first is to focus on a feature of your product—one that is different or unique, and that delivers an important benefit to the user. Examples:

1. Crispix cereal. The manufacturer didn't say it "tasted better." They said Crispix "stays crisp in milk"—a benefit consumers wanted.

2. Wonder Bread. "Helps build strong bodies twelve ways." They didn't say it was better tasting or more nutritious. They just said Wonder Bread built strong bodies in twelve ways.

The second way to create a unique selling proposition with selling power is to narrow the target market; that is, to focus on a specific market niche. For example, there are thousands of business consultants out there, all fighting for clients. But my old high school chum, Gary Gerber, is a consultant who doesn't fight for clients. He has all he can handle and potential clients waiting in line to hire him. Why? Because he is not just a business development consultant. He is a business development consultant specializing in eye doctors. It doesn't hurt that, before becoming a business development consultant to eye doctors, he owned the largest and most successful optometry practice in New Jersey. If you were an eye doctor looking to build your practice, who would you want to work with—Gary or a consultant who says he can help you but has never worked with an eye doctor before?

The third way to create a winning USP is with branding. The branding approach usually takes a massive, costly advertising campaign that small businesses cannot afford, although there are ways to shortcut this, such as with a celebrity spokesperson. A great example is the George Foreman grill. This is clearly not the world's best grill, nor do I recall the manufacturer making this claim in their commercials. But it is the *only* grill you can buy with the name George Foreman on it. So if you want a grill that cooks good food, you can get it lots of places. But if you want a George Foreman grill, you can *only* get it from the George Foreman grill company.

You can't confidently promote and sell yourself without a strong universal selling proposition. After all, if you don't have the reason why someone should buy your product instead of competing products at the tip of your tongue how will you persuade prospects to buy what you're selling instead of going to your competitors? When formulating a USP, start by asking yourself these questions:

1. What is different about my product that delivers an important benefit to the user?

2. Is there an industry, application, or other niche I can specialize in?

3. Is there a way to brand my company or product in a unique fashion with appeal to consumers?

Examples of classic USPs include:

(1) "It melts in your mouth, not in your hands." (M&M)

(2) "Good to the last drop." (Maxwell House)

(3) "You deserve a break today." (McDonald's)

But how do you know whether your universal selling proposition is any good and whether it will stand up in the marketplace? In his 1960 book, "Reality in Advertising," Rosser Reeves introduced the notion of a universal selling proposition, and he said that, to be successful, a USP must satisfy three criteria. To quote Reeves directly:

1. Each advertisement must make a proposition to the consumer. Each advertisement must say to the reader, "Buy this product, and you will get this specific benefit."

2. The proposition must be one that the competition either cannot, or does not, offer. It must be unique—either a uniqueness of brand or a claim not otherwise made in that particular field.

3. The proposition must be so strong that it can move the mass millions, i.e., pull over new customers to your product.

Never mind that many USPs today seem to violate these three guidelines. There are exceptions to all rules, of course. And you could get lucky by just winging it. But why take the risk? Your greatest odds of success come from adhering to Reeves' guidelines and making sure your USP is as strong as it can be. See whether your USP meets all three guidelines:

1. "Each advertisement must make a proposition to the consumer. Each advertisement must say to the reader: 'Buy this product, and you will get this specific benefit.'" Strong USPs have a benefit, either direct or implied. Weak ones don't. State Farm's "Like a good neighbor, State Farm is there" has a benefit: if you have a problem and are insured by State Farm, they will review and pay your claim promptly, giving you the money you need sooner. Nike's "Just do it" has no benefit. Therefore, it fails the test.

2. "The proposition must be one that the competition either cannot, or does not, offer. It must be unique—either a uniqueness of brand or a claim not otherwise made in that particular field." Here's where the 'unique' in unique selling proposition comes in. To differentiate yourself from the competition, it's not enough just to offer a benefit; you have to offer something that your competition either cannot or does not. As the first chocolate to feature a hard shell coating, M&M achieved their unique positioning with "melts in your mouth, not in your hand"—something only they could claim. Yes, other hard-coated candies followed. But by then, M&M already owned the position. What would these candies say? "We *also* melt in your mouth, not in your hand"?

Note that Reeves says the claim does not have to be a unique feature your competition cannot offer. It can also be something your competition *does* not offer, "a claim not otherwise made" in that field. The classic example is the story in Claude Hopkins Scientific Advertising of the ad campaign for a beer. The ad agency copywriter noticed that the bottles were washed in live steam, and commented to the brewery master, who replied, "That's nothing; everyone does that."

"But the beer-drinking public does not know that!" countered the copywriter, who went on to write a successful campaign based on the idea, "Beer so pure, the bottles are washed in live steam!"

3. "The proposition must be so strong that it can move the mass millions, i.e., pull over new customers to your product." A common mistake in promoting technology is to build some minor, insignificant difference into the product, and then tell the prospect that only you have it. Since the difference is in fact minor and insignificant, the market's reaction is likely to be, "Yes, you have it. But who cares?" Make sure the difference you are promoting—the 'unique' in unique selling proposition—delivers a benefit or performance difference that the reader really cares about, one that creates a significant advantage over other products in the category. For instance, a copywriter touring a piano factory noticed that a metal bar was installed in each piano. The factory foreman explained, "Wood warps over time. The bar stabilizes the piano to prevent warping. That way, this piano will sound the same twenty years from now the same as it does the day it is first played." That unique feature, the stabilizer bar, coupled with a powerful benefit—preservation of sound quality—became the basis for a successful ad campaign.

CHAPTER 51

Overcoming Reader Skepticism with the *Secondary Promise*

"Promise, large promise, is the soul of an advertisement," wrote Samuel Johnson. Today we know he was right: to break through the clutter and generate a profitable response, direct marketing must make a big promise. Some examples of big promises from recent direct mail packages:

1. "Retire overseas on $600 a month."

2. "Free money reserved for you."

3. "John F. Kennedy had it. So did Princess Diana. Michael Jordan has it now. It's the reason why millions of people adore them. Look inside to find out what it is and how you can get it."

Testing shows that, at least in consumer direct marketing, small promises don't work. To get attention and generate interest, you have to make a large, powerful promise. But there's a problem: what happens if the reader is skeptical because the big promise is so fantastic it sounds too good to be true? In that case, use a *secondary promise*.

The secondary promise is a lesser benefit that the product also delivers. Although not as large as the big promise, the secondary promise should be big enough so that, by itself, it is reason enough to order the product, yet small enough so that it is easily believed. This way, even if the readers are totally skeptical about the big promise, they can believe the secondary promise and order on that basis alone.

For instance, a recent investment promotion had a big promise in its headline: "Crazy as it Sounds, Shares of This Tiny R&D Company, Selling for $2 Today, Could be Worth as Much as $100 in the Not-Too-Distant Future." That's a really big promise—having a stock go from $2 to $100 is a gain of 4,900 percent. On a thousand shares, your profit would be $98,000. The problem is, in a bear market, this gain may, to some readers, be too high to be believable. Yet, in this case, it was the truth. If the company's medical device won FDA approval, a fifty-fold increase in share price was not out of the question.

The solution: a subhead, placed directly under the big promise in the headline, made a secondary promise: "I think this new technology for treating liver disease is going to work. And if it does, the stock price could easily increase fifty-fold or more. But even if it doesn't—and the company's treatment is a total failure—the stock could still earn early-stage investors a five-hundred percent gain on their shares within the next twenty-four months." The catch was this: even if the treatment did not win FDA approval, the company would still make a lot of money (thought not as much as with the treatment being approved) using the same technology in a different application. So even if the big promise didn't pan out, the secondary promise was enough to make the stock worth owning.

There are many techniques you can use to prove your big promise when your reader is skeptical. These include testimonials, case studies, test results, favorable reviews, superior product design, track record, system or methodology, and reputation of the manufacturer. All are good. But the trouble is this: if the big promise is so strong that readers are inclined to dismiss it as false, you find yourself arguing with them and going against their ingrained belief when you introduce all this proof. I would still present the proof, but an easier way to overcome doubt concerning the big promise is to always accompany it with a secondary promise that is desirable yet smaller and more credible.

The secondary promise is your back-up promise. In a package with both a big promise and a secondary promise, the big promise will attract readers because it is so large—and if you offer enough proof, many of those readers will believe it.

What about those prospects who are not convinced? Without a secondary promise, they simply toss your mailing without responding. But when you add a secondary promise and make it prominent (which means featuring it in the headline or the lead), many of those who reject the big promise as being unbelievable will find the secondary promise credible and appealing enough to sell them all on its own.

Actually, with a secondary promise, prospects who don't fully believe your big promise can still be sold by it. They think, "Hey, if this big promise happens to be true, this is a good product to buy; but even if it isn't true, the product is more than worth the price just for the secondary promise, which I am sure *is* true by itself. So either way, I can't lose." And if you use both a big promise and a secondary promise in your next promotion, neither can you. And that's a promise.

Part VII
Trade Show Marketing

CHAPTER 52

Are Trade Shows Worth Your Time and Money?

Every year, industry spends more than seven billion dollars to exhibit its wares at trade shows and expositions throughout the country. There are more than nine thousand shows each year, so you can be sure there's a show specializing in whatever it is you do. There are shows for everything from chemicals to construction, from farm equipment to pharmaceuticals, from textiles to telecommunications.

At first glance, it seems as if exhibiting at trade shows is too expensive for a small company. And there's some truth to that at least where the major national shows are concerned. For example, when you consider the cost of travel, lodging, shipping, space, and materials, a manufacturer in Wichita could easily spend ten thousand dollars on a ten-foot booth at the Computer Sales Exposition in New York City. Obviously, continent hopping is beyond the budgets of most small businesses (and it makes little sense for a Kansas-based firm to exhibit in New York unless the company is large enough to distribute nationwide).

But there are alternatives: regional shows; tabletop shows; county fairs; state fairs; public shows; chamber of commerce exhibitions; and thousands of other small, local shows that make sense for small business. The questions are: Where do you find out about these shows? And how do you pick the ones that are right for you?

Choosing the right trade show is like selecting advertising media or publicity outlets. You pick the places that let you reach the most prospects at the lowest possible cost. Begin with a comprehensive listing of local and national shows. One such listing is *Exhibit Schedule,* published by Successful Meetings magazine, 1422 Chestnut Street, Philadelphia, PA 19102. Another is *Trade Show Convention Guide,* available from Budd Publications, Box 7, New York, NY 10004. Trade journals and business publications will include monthly listings of shows and conferences in your particular industry. And your local convention and exhibit bureau can give you the latest information on fairs and expos in your city or town. From these listings, you'll glean perhaps a dozen or so shows where you might exhibit because they're local, or because they are applicable to your type of business. Write to the management of each of these shows, and ask for a prospectus or other literature. You'll want to know how many people are expected to attend the show, how many have attended past shows, where these people come from, what industries they represent, what job titles they hold. In short, are they the type of people that want, need, and can afford to buy your products?

Are your competitors exhibiting? That's one sure sign that the show may be worth attending. Is the show a new one, or is it well established? Select those shows that have proven their worth over time. Too many fly-by-night expos spring up one year and are gone the next. And the companies that invest in them are usually thousands of dollars poorer for their efforts.

CHAPTER 53

How to Design a Great Display

Assuming that you sign up for a schedule of trade shows, what will you display there and why? The most compelling reason for your company to participate in a trade show is to introduce a new product to the marketplace. According to studies by the Trade Show Bureau, fifty percent of the people attending any given show are there to see new products and services. So if you've invented the better mousetrap, motor, or metal detector, a trade show may be the place to show it off. But if you're selling the same old thing, avoid trade shows and try some other promotion, such as a trade ad or direct mail campaign.

What is the best way to get people to notice your new product? Demonstrate it. To your prospects, seeing new products in action is the main reason for going to shows. Live action is the one thing that separates a show from print promotions. At trade shows, attendees can see your product, touch it, feel it, smell it, and compare it with the competitor whose booth may be right next to your own. Prospects can't discuss product features with an advertisement; printed pages don't answer when questions are asked. But at the show, buyers see whether your orange juice machine really can squeeze five gallons an hour, or whether it filters out the pulp. And if they want to ask what kind of price break they can get if they buy juicers in bulk, they can get a straight answer from a real live salesperson right then and there.

Unfortunately, straightforward demonstrations can produce more yawns than inquiries, since most products and equipment are—let's face it—just plain boring. (Ever hear of someone flying three hundred miles to see a sump pump in action?) If your product is nuts and bolts, make the demonstration a little less mundane by adding a touch of flair to the display. For example, a defense contractor was exhibiting helicopters at an Air Force show. In the middle of the display area was the hull of a chopper that had been struck point blank by an enemy missile. Its windshield was cracked, its armor plating buckled by the impact, but that was all. The helicopter had survived the attack. And so, a huge sign taped to the windshield told us, did its two pilots. That is a most impressive display, combining drama with convincing product demonstration.

You don't have to be selling weapons to set up an interesting, unusual product demonstration that will bring the crowds swarming to your booth. One small manufacturer of scuba equipment built a huge Plexiglas fish tank for their booth. The tank was about eight feet high and six feet wide, and inside it swam a bikini-clad beauty who stayed underwater all day, aided by—you guessed it—the exhibitor's marvelous scuba gear. Cost of the tank? About eight hundred dollars, less than a third the cost of placing a full-page ad in a trade journal. The results? A booth jam packed with prospects looking at a demonstration that was the hit of the show.

Want to get people to take a look at your orange juice squeezer? Offer a glass of fresh squeezed juice to everybody who stops by to take a peek. Are passersby passing by your display of home video games? Get them to stop and take notice by challenging them to beat the highest score on your newest computer game and by giving free game cartridges to the top ten players. Selling a minicomputer that works like magic? Have a professional magician on hand to demonstrate its features in a magical way.

As with any promotion, the first step in successful trade shows is getting the prospect's attention. Product demonstrations, giveaways, contests, and entertainment are four attention grabbers that will pull people from the aisle into your booth. And that's where the selling starts.

CHAPTER 54

Train Your Salespeople to Staff the Booth

Retailers may take orders at the show, but the bulk of trade show exhibitors in manufacturing don't. Instead, they use shows to introduce new products or new applications of old products. They use shows to make contacts, build prospect lists, be seen by decision makers, talk to customers and distribute sales literature.

Trade shows are an unusual hybrid of advertising and personal selling. Advertising, because you pay for a space (in the case of a show, it's an actual space on the floor) and personal selling, because once the display attracts the prospect to the booth, the salesperson has to do the rest. So, although this is a book on marketing, not salesmanship, we're going to take a brief look at personal selling as it applies to the trade show.

To begin with, picture this scene: the prospect, attracted by the flashing lights, bells, whistles, and sirens of your product demonstration, walks toward the booth. You say, "May I help you?" The prospect's reply? A hastily muttered, "No thank you" followed by a quick exit away from your booth. "May I help you?" —the standard department store lead-in—is the worst way to introduce yourself. If the prospects are not intimately familiar with what you're selling (and chances are they're not) they will feel threatened by this challenge and it will scare them off. Instead, draw your prospects into conversation by asking friendly, non-threatening questions about business; general questions. If you're selling globe valves to petroleum engineers, don't say, "Are you thinking of buying our Model X-100 valve?" Instead, ask, "Do you specify valves in your work?" A "no" answer means you're not talking with a qualified prospect; a "yes" tells you to keep the conversation going. Then find out the prospect's problem. And discuss and show how your product can solve that problem. Get chummy. Glance at the prospects' badges or ID tags so you can address them by name. Be personal, friendly and helpful—but not pushy.

A cardinal rule of trade show selling: Stay on your feet. People will not disturb you if you're resting your rear in a chair or on a stool. You can't sell if you're seated, so stand. If you need a rest, have someone take your place while you walk around the exhibit hall or stop at the snack bar, but no napping in the booth, please.

Another cardinal rule of trade show selling: Don't gab with friends and fellow employees when you're manning the booth. Strangers will not interrupt a conversation between friends. Instead, they will pass you by and stop at a display where the sales help isn't occupied. Need to chat with the boss or your assistant for a few minutes? Find a nice quiet corner outside of the display area.

A question we get asked frequently is: "Should we hand out our brochure to everyone who asks for it?" Well, there are pros and cons to this practice. The pro of having literature on hand is that you can quickly satisfy a prospect's hunger for more information. And the brochure serves as a permanent reminder of his visit to your booth. On the con side, sales literature is costly to produce, and handing out a fancy four-color brochure to thousands of people, regardless of whether they're serious sales prospects, can be an expensive proposition. The alternative—not having literature at the show—also has its pros and cons. Without a large supply of brochures, you will have to take down the names and addresses of the people who request information in order to mail the literature at a later date.

Many shows issue each attendee a plastic show card much like a credit card. When the attendee hands you the card, you use a special imprinter, also supplied by show management, to instantly record the sales lead on preprinted forms. This technique can work to your advantage, allowing you to build a list of prospects who have expressed interest in your product. A negative is that you've now got to mail thousands of brochures, where before, literature was there for the taking. Also, this system delays getting the brochure into the buyer's hands and that could hurt sales if the buyers are in a hurry.

Here's our solution: Keep a small sampling of your literature on a table or in a display rack in open view for everyone to see. If a prospect wants a brochure, take down the information and mail it later if, in your judgment, the prospect means business. If you think the person's just collecting brochures, then you can note this on the lead form or their business card, and mail the literature or not, as you choose. Behind the display or under the table, you'll have a surplus supply of several hundred brochures on hand. These are to be distributed to hot prospects who are really serious about your product and want to get down to business right away. With a little practice, you'll be able to tell the buyers from the brochure collectors without a second glance.

Finally, a few more tips to improve your trade show selling:

1. Develop a schedule for staffing the booth. Even the most energetic salesperson will get tired, cranky, and bored after eight hours of standing in a ten by ten foot display filled with file cabinets or fishing poles. Let your salespeople man the booth in two-hour or four-hour rotation shifts, so prospects are always greeted by a salesperson who's relatively fresh and lively. Naturally, the busier the traffic (flow of people through your booth), the more booth personnel you'll need. Plan the booth duty roster accordingly. Experience teaches us that shows are busy during the middle days, and slower during their start and finish. As an example of this, take

a look at the attendance figures for the Exposition of Chemical Industries:

Day one: 4,341 attendees

Day two: 5,417 attendees

Day three: 6,016 attendees

Day four: 2,850 attendees.

2. Reduce prices on products sold at the show. The opportunity to pick up merchandise at reduced cost gives prospects a reward for having taken the time and trouble to visit your display.

3. Use pre-show promotion to build booth traffic. Use advertising, publicity, and direct mail to get prospects to come to the show. For a nominal cost, show management will provide artwork, stickers, mail stuffers, and invitations you can use in your own promotions. This material can easily and inexpensively be imprinted with your company logo and the number of your booth. Include an imprinted show invitation with invoices, literature mailings, personal letters, and other day-to-day correspondence. And don't forget to mention the show in your ads.

Part VIII

Other Marketing Tactics

CHAPTER 55

Are Customer Surveys an Absolute Waste of Time?

It sounds like a good idea: survey customers to find out what they want, and then let their answers shape your product development and marketing. But in reality, it's often a bust.

A case in point: according to an article in *BusinessWeek* (August 1, 2005, page 38), in 2002, the Gap began an intensive program of focus groups, surveys, and other market research. But in the fiscal quarter ending April 30, 2005, sales fell four percent. Analysts expected them to drop another two percent for the quarter ending on July 30, 2005. The reason: eight former employees and two analysts say, "the Gap has shifted too far toward research and away from the instinct and emotion favored by many successful clothing merchandisers."

I see an insidious trend today, especially among traditional marketers turning toward direct marketing: they sincerely believe they can, through customer surveys, confirm that consumers will respond to the product, price, offer, headline, and copy before producing and mailing the promotion. They mistakenly believe that if they get enough survey responses, they are guaranteed a winning promotion simply by stringing the consumer responses together into copy. Unfortunately, experienced direct marketers know that there is a huge gap between what consumers *say* they will buy and what they actually buy. And for this reason, the only accurate way to determine what will sell is through testing: selling a real product with a real offer to real consumers who vote their preferences not by answering a survey, but with their purchases.

"In my 10 plus years experience in direct marketing publishing, I've found that customer surveys can be very misleading," says 'Julie,' a blogger responding to my blog site. "Recipients tend to give answers they think you want to hear. Case in point: a company spent over $100,000 developing a product that customer survey respondents said they would purchase. At the end of the day, they didn't purchase. And the company lost a bundle. My advice: treat survey responses as minor gauges of interest. Tread lightly. And test, test, test!"

"A lot of the time customers really don't know what they want," says 'Peter,' another blogger. "The masses simply clamor about waiting for the next best thing. Not exactly the best group of folks to ask. This kind of thing permeates video game design discussions quite frequently. Everyone wants to predict what the next blockbuster title will be based on current trends, when in reality, you could spend millions of dollars on focus groups of current title enthusiasts and come up with an ultra-generic flop."

Copywriter Steve Slaunwhite relates this experience, "A few years ago an insurance company hired me to create a direct mail package. When the design and copy were completed to draft form, my client had a brilliant idea: 'Let's show this to a focus group of potential customers,'" the client said. "Nothing I said could dissuade him," continued Steve. "Based on feedback from the group, my client made sweeping changes to the package, which included eliminating all references to the word *free*. ' Too trite,' they said. The package was mailed. And it flopped. What went wrong? Not the focus group, according to my client. 'The focus group can't be wrong,' he asserts. 'After all, they're the customers!'"

One reason that customer surveys are particularly ineffective for evaluating promotional copy is that consumers like to believe they are immune to direct marketing techniques. A focus group will loudly proclaim that your 'buy one, get one free offer' won't work with them because they don't like gimmicks. Then, in an actual test, that same offer will perform like gangbusters, beating the pants off the straightforward offer the focus group members all said they preferred.

So the next time someone at your company says "Let's do a customer survey," keep these facts in mind:

1. Survey results are not terribly accurate predictors of what products and offers will sell, the price consumers will pay, or the headlines, copy, or promotions to which they will respond.

2. Surveys, in particular focus groups, *are* useful for discovering the language that consumers use to talk about a particular product, need, or problem.

3. The Internet allows large numbers of consumers to be surveyed quickly and at low cost, with online tools such as www.surveymonkey.com.

CHAPTER 56

Write and Design
Better Sales Brochures

When I was the advertising manager for a process equipment manufacturer, one of my responsibilities was to serve as liaison between the advertising agency we hired to write our ads and product brochures and our staff engineers. The engineers, because of their technical expertise in the subject matter, were responsible for reviewing the agency's work. As is often the case in our industry, the engineers complained that those 'ad types' at the agency didn't understand the product or the audience, and that their copy was way off base. The agency countered that engineers may know technology but don't know writing, marketing, design, or selling—and that they wanted to cram the brochures with too much unnecessary detail that would dilute the sales message. Who was right? The fact is that both arguments have some merit.

On the agency side, ad agency folk often have a flair for creative, colorful communication, which can help a brochure gain attention and be noticed. On the other hand, clients—especially the engineers who review the agency's brochure copy—often complain, sometimes correctly, that the agency's brochure copy is superficial. Laziness is often the cause. The writer did not do sufficient research to understand both the technology and the needs, concerns, and interests of the target audience. The copy he writes reflects this lack of understanding. When you read it, you immediately think, "This person doesn't know what he is talking about"—and you are probably right.

Another problem with professional or agency-written product literature is a tendency toward cleverness for the sake of being clever. "Be creative!" the client instructs the agency. But the readers often don't get the joke, pun, or reference in the headline, the creativity goes over their heads, and they are turned off rather than engaged.

Engineers who write their own brochure copy are rarely superficial; they usually have a solid understanding of the products and its technology. However, engineers tend to assume that the reader knows as much as the writer, speaks the same jargon, and has the same level of interest in the technology. And often this is not the case.

Consider the use of jargon. People today frequently use the term 'open systems architecture' in sales literature. But do they really know what this means? Write down your own definition, ask five colleagues to do the same, and compare. I guarantee they will not be the same. Engineers who write often don't strive for clarity. So they fall back on buzzwords and clichés that, unfortunately, don't get across the messages they wish to convey. Given these conditions, how can you—as an engineer or manager who either writes brochure copy, edits copy, approves copy, or provides input for ad agencies or freelance industrial copywriters—do your job better so the finished brochure is the best one possible? Here are some simple guidelines to follow:

1. *Define the topic.* Is your brochure about a solution? A system? A product line? A product? A specific model of that product? A specific industry use or application of that product? The support services you offer for that product? The accessories? Define what the piece is *about*. The narrower the topic, the more focused, specific, and effective your brochure can be within the limited space available. Tip: your brochure doesn't have to cover everything. You

can always decide to have other pieces of sales literature that go into more depth on certain aspects of the product. For instance, you can talk about satisfied users in case histories. You can expand on specifications in a spec sheet. Some marketers use application briefs to focus on a specific application or industry. Others develop separate sell sheets on each key feature, allowing more in-depth technical discussion than is possible in a general product brochure.

2. *Know your audience.* Are you writing to engineers or managers? The former may be interested in technical and performance specifications. The latter may want to know about support, service, ease of use, scalability, user benefits, or return on investment. If you are writing to engineers, are they well versed in this particular technology? Or do you have to bring them up to speed? Just because someone is a chemical engineer does not mean they know nearly as much about industrial knives, turbine blades, corrosion-resistant metals, ball valves, or your particular specialty as you do; indeed, they probably don't. When in doubt, it is better to explain so everyone understands than to assume that everyone already understands. No engineer has ever complained to me that a brochure I wrote was too clear.

3. *Write with your objective in mind.* Unlike a Victoria's Secrets catalog, which gives the buyer all the information needed to place an order, most technical product brochures support the selling process but are not designed to complete it on their own. Is the objective of the brochure to convince the prospect that your technical design is superior to your competition? Or show that you have more features at a better price? Or demonstrate that your system will pay back its cost in less than six months? Establish a communication objective for the brochure and write with that goal in mind. For instance, if the objective is to get a meeting for you to sell consulting services to the client, you only need to include enough to convince them that the meeting is worth their time. Anything more is probably overkill.

4. *Include the two things every brochure should contain.* These simply are: (a) the things your prospects need and want to know about your product to make their buying decision and (b) what you think you should say to persuade them that your product is the best product choice—and your company is the best vendor. The things a prospect wants to know about an industrial product might include weight, dimensions, power requirements, operating temperature, and whether it can perform certain functions. Things you might want to tell them include how the performance compares with competitive systems in benchmark tests (if you were the winner, of course) or the fact that it was cited as a 'Best Product' by an industry publication, or won an award from a trade association, or is the most popular product in its category with an installed base of more than ten thousand units.

5. *Be selective.* While ad agency copy is sometimes too light and tells the reader too little, engineer copy often makes the opposite error, attempting to cram every last technical fact and feature into a four or eight page brochure. Keep in mind that your prospects are bombarded by more information than they can handle on a daily basis. Everyone has too much to read, and not enough time to read it. According to a study by the School of Information Management & Systems at the University of California—Berkeley, each year the human race produces about 1.5 exabytes of unique information in print, film, optical, and magnetic content worldwide—roughly 250MB of new information for every man, women, and child. Be selective in your presentation. Copywriter Herschell Gordon Lewis has a formula, $E^2 = 0$. Or, as Lewis says, "When you emphasize everything, you emphasize nothing." If every fact about your product is given equal weight in the brochure, the key facts that make the most persuasive case for buying the product will not stand out.

6. *Understand the selling environment.* There are three basic selling situations for process equipment, chemicals, and other in-

dustrial products. You must know what situation your product falls into, so you can market it effectively. The first situation is that the prospects are not acutely aware of the problem he has that your product can solve. Or they are aware of it but do not consider it a priority. In this situation, to get your prospects' attention, your brochure must dramatize the problem and its severity, and then position your product as the solution. Example: Mainframe computer operators did not realize that certain operations accidentally overrode and erased files stored on magnetic tapes. A brochure for a utility that prevented this operation from occurring began, "Did you know that your storage devices may be accidentally wiping out important files even as you read this sentence?" It alerted them to the problem in a dramatic way. Once alerted to a problem they didn't know existed, the readers were eager to find a solution, which the utility handily provided. Sales were brisk.

The second situation is that the prospects are aware of the problem or need your product addresses, but are not at all convinced that your type of product is the best solution. Example: a chemical manufacturer warned wastewater treatment plants that their current activated charcoal bed systems were too costly. The plant managers believed that, but didn't believe that the manufacturer's alternative filter technology was a viable solution. A paper reprinting lab test results plus the offer of a free trial overcame the disbelief and got firms to use the new filter system.

The third situation is when the prospects know what their problem is, believe your type of product is the right solution, but need to be convinced that your product is the best choice in the category, and better than similar products offered by your competitors. One way to demonstrate superiority is with a table comparing your product with the others on a feature-by-feature basis. If you have a more complete feature set than they do, such a table makes you look like the best choice.

Another technique is to give specifications that prove your performance is superior. If this cannot be quantitatively measured, talk about any unique functionality, technology, or design feature that might create an impression of superiority in the prospect's mind.

There are many other copywriting techniques available to produce a superior technical product brochure in any of these three situations; this is why I've devoted the past twenty-five years, my entire professional life, to practicing and studying copywriting—just like an engineer practices and studies his specialty. But if you follow these basics and do nothing else, I guarantee an improvement in your brochures that you, your sales reps, and your customers will appreciate. You might even some day receive that rare compliment: "You know, I actually read your brochure. It wasn't boring, and it told me what I needed to know!"

CHAPTER 57

Yellow Pages Advertising

Here's one Yellow Pages advertising technique that may work for you. Ironically, I learned it from my dad. I say ironically because my father had no interest in advertising or marketing. His expertise was insurance—he was an insurance agent, and he knew the technical aspects of insurance inside and out. He ran a one-man insurance agency in downtown Paterson using his own name—"F.W. 'Dave' Bly Insurance." The *F* stood for Fabian, which he hated. Most people who hate their first names go by their middle name—but the *W* in *F.W.* stood for Wolf, which he equally despised. He told me that when he was a kid and he met new kids who asked him his name, he would mumble "Fabe"—short for Fabian—and hope they couldn't hear him clearly. One day, another kid replied, "Did you say 'Dave'?" "Yeah," said dad, and from then on he went by Dave—for the rest of his life.

His major means of advertising his agency was an ad in the Yellow Pages. As a small independent agent in the rather downscale city of Paterson, NJ, where we lived, Dave Bly couldn't afford the biggest ad on the page; other, larger agencies could always outspend him. So one year he decided to try something new. In his small display ad (I can't remember the exact size), he made the headline **"INSURANCE"** in large, bold type. Underneath, he had two columns of bullets—a laundry list of all the types of items he could insure for you. In the list, he focused on items that people frequently asked about but that other insurance agents did not actively pursue. Snowmobiles, I recall, were one of the items in his bullet list. Underneath he had the name of his agency and the phone number. Well, that bullet list ad was far more successful than any other ad he ever ran, getting him at least one phone call a day from people needing insurance. They told him they were trying to find insurance for a particular item (like a snowmobile). So they opened the Yellow Pages to 'insurance,' and his ad was the only insurance ad in the book with the word 'snowmobiles' in it. So of course they called him first. Other agents, of course, could also insure snowmobiles and the other items in his bullet list. But if you want to buy a kiwi fruit, which ad will you respond to—the one that says 'fruits' or the one that says 'kiwis'?

Consumer Reports used this technique in a recent mailing to sell subscriptions to their magazine. The magazine rates consumer products in a wide variety of categories for quality. Many people, however, think of Consumer Reports primarily for their new car ratings. A recent mailing used an oversize envelope. Printed on the outer envelope were the names of dozens of consumer products covered by Consumer Reports—everything from loudspeakers and soy milk, to treadmills and microwave ovens. Literally dozens of different products listed.

Dad never made a fortune as an insurance agent, but he took himself out of poverty (he was a child during the Great Depression) and supported a family of four—and his Yellow Pages ads always paid back their cost many times over. He was a patriotic American, but not a rabid capitalist—he felt insurance costs were getting out of control and that the only way to make it affordable to the masses would eventually be to socialize insurance. He would often say of the insurance industry, "Insurance companies want to write fire insurance policies for pig iron at the bottom of the ocean." He was also old-fashioned: computers came into insurance offices, but by then, he was near the end of his career and refused to learn them, never even touching a PC. He left the PC work to his assistant, who, by that time, was my mother and who, now recently retired, has a computer in her home.

CHAPTER 58

What Donald Trump Can Teach You about Direct Marketing

I never thought of Donald Trump as a direct marketer. In fact, from what little I had seen, he seemed largely ignorant of the principles of direct marketing. For instance, on the first season of *The Apprentice*, the two teams had to each come up with an ad campaign for a company that made corporate jets (complete with flight crew) available to clients who wanted to fly in private jets, but did not have the budget to buy their own. Trump praised one team's campaign which featured slick color photos of various parts of the jet shot at angles that made them look like phallic symbols. "Idiot!" I complained to my wife, who was also watching. "The ads should have offered a Membership Card entitling the recipient to get the first thirty minutes of any flight free!" (That's how we direct marketers think—offer, offer, offer.)

But a recent episode in the second season of *The Apprentice* was much more encouraging in its demonstration of direct response principles. This time, two teams each had the task of putting together and running, for one evening only, a bridal shop in New York City. The content was simple: whichever team had the highest gross sales for the evening would be the winner. Team *A* printed huge stacks of pink fliers inviting people to the sale. They distributed these fliers by handing them out at Penn Station as morning commuters got off the trains to make their way to work. Trump correctly questioned the wisdom of Team *A*'s marketing strategy, asking, "How many people are thinking about getting married when they're commuting to work in the morning?"

Team *B* took a more targeted approach: they rented an e-list of thousands of women who were planning to get married and emailed them an invitation to the bridal sale. I think you can guess the result. Team *A* had only a handful of customers in their shop, sold only two dresses, and grossed around one thousand dollars. Team *B* had customers lining up on the sidewalk to get into the store as if it were an exclusive Manhattan nightclub. They sold twenty-six dresses for gross revenues of more than twelve thousand dollars, outselling Team *B* more than twelve to one.

The project manager of Team *A* was fired by Trump that night. The lesson for direct marketers is clear: the list is all-important. In this case, Team *B* knew that everyone on their list was planning to get married. Team *A*, by comparison, handed out their invitation to anyone and everyone at Penn Station. How many of those people had any interest in getting married? Was it one out of a hundred, or maybe one out of a thousand? This 'list' used by Team *A* had maybe ninety to ninety-nine percent wasted circulation, meaning the promotion went to the wrong people: those not interested in buying the product. The list used by Team *B* had maybe one percent or as little as zero percent wasted circulation, because virtually everyone on the list had indicated a planned wedding. And the result? *B* out pulled *A* by approximately twelve to one, a differential that is not uncommon in actual direct marketing tests. This means using the best mailing list versus the worst mailing list can increase your response rates one thousand percent or more, which makes testing different mailing lists perhaps the best marketing investment you can make this year—well—next to getting on *The Apprentice*.

CHAPTER 59

Promote Yourself
by Writing Articles

Recently DD, a top copywriter, emailed me for some advice about using articles as a marketing tool. "An editor has contacted me about doing an article," wrote DD. "Seems like a good opportunity to generate some publicity for my product and some nice credentials for myself. Do you have any advice or precautions, like how to maximize this opportunity, or things I might not know to consider when writing a magazine article to promote myself and my business?" Here's what I told DD.

To begin with, just because an editor wants you to write an article does not mean you should. If you're writing articles for free as a promotional vehicle, only write for two types of publications. The first is publications whose readers are the target market for your product or service. The second is publications so prestigious that your prospects will be impressed by the credential of you having published in their pages. Now, even though you're writing the article to promote yourself, don't promote yourself in the article. The only way your article is going to build your reputation and get people interested in doing business with you is with solid content, not self-promotional blather. Focus on the reader and the topic and not on you.

For instance, if you're a consultant, you can give little vignettes in your article about how businesspeople applied smart management principles to solve problems. But don't take the credit. Say instead, "Ned, a manager at XYZ company," and describe what he did. Don't say, "When Ned called me in, here is what I did," even if you were responsible. Give credit to others, and play down your own role in the stories your articles contain. This way, you come off as modest and not as a blatant self-promoter, which quickly turns people off.

Give your readers useful hints and tips about your topic—short, practical, pithy advice on how to do their jobs or run their lives better. When they read your sage advice, they will nod their heads in recognition of your wisdom and begin to think of you as their guru on this topic. The only promotion or 'advertising' should appear in the About the Author box that usually runs at the bottom of the first column of the article when it's published in the magazine. Your About the Author copy should say who you are, what you do, and how to contact you. That means including an email address or website, or both.

As for length, ask the editor. He or she will usually tell you how many words are desired. Stick to that count. Once the article is published, the contact information in your About the Author box will generate some response for you. But don't leave it at that. Make your article do double or triple duty as a promotional tool. You can:

1. Make reprints of your article.

2. Include copies of your article in the inquiry fulfillment kits you mail to potential customers.

3. Hand out article reprints at trade shows.

4. Do a mailing of your article reprint to your clients and prospects.

5. Post the articles on your website. Having lots of content on your site makes visitors stay longer—and also raises your rankings with search engines.

If the response is good and your article seems to have reached the right people (your target market), immediately send an email to your editor. Suggest a follow-up article with information you didn't have room to include in the first article.

If you like to write and have the time (or you can hire a ghost-writer), why not suggest a monthly column in the magazine instead of just an article? The worst the editor can do is say no. If the editor says yes, you'll get your name in front of your potential customers twelve times a year instead of once. And, you'll accelerate your recognition as a top expert in your field. Those are great results from one of the easiest self-promotions you can do: writing articles.

CHAPTER 60

Promote Your Business Through Public Speaking

One of the ways in which you can market your product or service is through public speaking. For instance, you'll often see financial seminars advertised in your local newspaper. The ads invite you to come for a lunch or evening seminar, typically just an hour or two, on a topic like estate planning, retirement planning, mutual funds, or some other aspect of personal finance or investing. The seminar, sponsored by a local brokerage, financial planner, or other financial services firm, is free. So how do they make money? By converting some of the attendees to their free seminar into paid clients for whom they manage money, prepare estate plans, or provide other financial services.

This 'give a free talk' strategy can work in many fields and venues. A consultant who specializes in small business management and marketing, for example, might speak at a Chamber of Commerce lunch to promote his services and sign up local business owners as clients. You can speak at local association lunches and dinners—the YMCA or YMHA, high school and college adult education programs, local libraries, trade shows and conferences.

So, why don't more entrepreneurs use the give a free talk promotional strategy? One reason is that the idea of speaking in front of a group makes them nervous. We often hear about surveys showing the number one fear of Americans to be public speaking . . .

ahead of flying, heights (my particular bugaboo), snakes, or even death. Now, I have been using the give a free talk strategy to promote myself as a freelance copywriter for more than two decades. And I've developed a technique that can help you deliver a superior presentation and overcome your butterflies at the same time. It's really simple, and you've already been doing it your whole life. It's called 'having a conversation with another person.'

You, along with virtually everyone else on the planet, are already an experienced and accomplished speaker. You speak all the time, every day, almost nonstop—to colleagues, coworkers, customers, supervisors, vendors, suppliers, friends, family, the clerk at the drug store, the waiter at the restaurant—in one-to-one personal conversations. Having these conversations comes naturally. You don't get nervous or scared. And, the people you talk to listen and respond, for the most part.

Well, to become a good speaker, all you need to do is have the same kind of one-to-one conversation with your audience when speaking in front of a group. When I am speaking to a group, I look into the audience as I begin talking, find one person who is looking back at me, and make eye contact. Then, I talk just to that one person as if we were having a private, one-on-one conversation. I know everyone else can hear us. But notice: I am not giving a lecture or making a speech, activities which the average person approaches with fear and trepidation. Instead, I am just having a conversation with one person. After a minute, I break eye contact, find another person in the audience, and make eye contact with them. I repeat this process throughout my talk. So I am never staring out into a crowd, seeing an ocean of bodies, which can be intimidating. Instead, I am always having a conversation with one person. The result? My fear and anxiety are totally gone and my presentation is much more conversational and natural than a stiff formal lecture or pontificating speech.

Here's one other tip: never bring your talk written out as a speech and read it word for word. Such presentations are stiff, unnatural, and boring. The listener knows you are reading a speech, and thinks, "This speaker could have just emailed me the talk to me as a PDF file and I could have read it at home without bothering to make the trip here."

Instead, outline your talk in bullet form. You can write the bullets on index cards for your eyes only. Or, put the major points on PowerPoint slides and project them in front of the audience so they can follow along with you. As a veteran of giving talks for more than a quarter-century, I think there are only a handful of other secrets. Let me share them with you.

1. *Know what you are talking about.* In Robert B. Parker's latest Spenser novel, *Cold Service*, Spenser says this to Susan about his sidekick Hawk: "He's nearly always right. Not because he knows everything. But because he never talks about things he doesn't know." This is a good tip for public speakers, bloggers, writers, and anyone else who communicates: stick to what you know and you'll be a more effective, more persuasive, more credible communicator. And by knowing a thing, I don't mean just researching and reading about it. I mean knowing from actual experience. The only way to ensure total credibility as a speaker is to not speak on a subject unless you've actually done it. If you haven't done it and an audience member challenges you, you are completely vulnerable because you don't totally know what you are talking about.

2. *Narrow the topic.* One of the biggest mistakes speakers make is to try to cover too much material in too short a time. The result is a rushed presentation that is either superficial—because no point can be covered in any meaningful way—or boring, because the information density is too high—there is too much for the listeners to absorb, and their eyes glaze over. The solution is to narrow your topic. For instance, "Safety" is too big and broad a topic to cover in a one-hour workshop, but "Ten Tips for Safe Handling of Compressed Cylinder Gases in the Plant," on the other hand, is manage-

able within a one-hour time frame.

3. *Organize your material.* One way to do this is to choose a title that dictates an organizational scheme to follow. If your title is "Safe Handling of Compressed Cylinder Gases in the Plant," you are then faced with deciding how to organize your content. The title dictates that the content is organized as a series of ten guidelines or suggestions. The "Ten Tips" has the added bonus of making attendees look forward to the talk; they become curious, and want to know what the ten tips are.

4. *Frame your talk.* This is an old formula that has been taught in public speaking classes for decades. The principle is, "Tell them what you're going to tell them. Tell them. And then tell them what you told them." If you are using PowerPoint, insert a slide between your title slide and the first slide of the material that says, "What we will cover today." Underneath that heading, list in bullets the main points to be covered on the remainder of the slides. After the last slide of content and before the closing slide (typically a logo, the speaker's contact information, or a call to action), insert a slide with the heading "To sum it all up." Underneath that heading, summarize the key points you made in the rest of the presentation.

The best book I ever read on giving talks is *Making Successful Presentations* (John Wiley & Sons), written by Terry C. Smith. Terry, my former boss at Westinghouse, has been teaching presentation skills for decades and is one of the best speakers I've ever heard. His book is out of print, but you can probably get it at www.alibris. com or on www.amazon.com. Another great book on speaking is *Talking to an Audience* by Vernon Howard, available from www. fourstarbooks.com.

When I wrote the above guidelines, I thought I had covered everything you need to know to be a really terrific speaker. But when I showed it to Terry Smith, he suggested a few more speaking tips for me to pass on to you.

1. *Rehearse*. Your presentation will never be great the first time you give it. So you want to give it many times before you're actually in front of your audience. That means rehearsing. You can rehearse by yourself ... or in front of your staff or family. Or, you can accept speaking gigs in venues that aren't critical to you (e.g., the local library or YMCA) before unveiling your talk to your target market—the people whose response really matters to you.

2. *Have something worthwhile for the audience*. In other words, show them how they will benefit from the advice or content in your talk. For instance, if your talk is announcing a new treatment for varicose veins, tell the audience about things they can do to prevent or relieve the symptoms of the condition, like mild exercise or wearing special stockings.

3. *Be yourself*. Avoid the well-meaning but misguided advice of speaking coaches and trainers who teach you theatrical techniques or tell you to change your manner, voice, and posture. Just be yourself. Audiences respond much more positively to real people than to mannequins and phonies.

4. *Be confident and positive*. Tell yourself, "I'm glad that I'm here, and I like what I'm doing"—even if it may not exactly be true. My experience is that, even if you don't like giving talks and don't look forward to doing them, once you step up to the lectern and open your mouth, your distaste will vanish and you'll gain enthusiasm.

OK. So now you have it: my complete mini-course on how to give a great talk. It really is everything you need to know about public speaking, which—as you can see—is not rocket science. Now, the next question is, how can you use this speaking to promote your business? I have a few suggestions.

1. *Get on the speaking schedule*. The most obvious is to find local meetings where the attendees are your potential clients, and offer to speak to them for free. There are thousands of meetings held each year throughout the country that routinely feature speakers at

luncheons and dinners. Since these small local groups don't have the budget to hire professional speakers, but want to deliver valuable content to their members, they are always on the lookout for speakers. It's not difficult to get on their schedule. Just send a letter to the person in charge of arranging for speakers. Mention your qualifications, the topic of your talk, and the key points you will cover. If it's relevant to the interests of the group, you'll get your opportunity to talk to the group.

Don't use this opportunity to deliver a speech that's a thinly disguised commercial or pitch for your services. Your audiences will hate such a talk and dislike you for giving it. And that won't produce the leads you want. The best way to get potential customers in the audience to want to do business with you is to give a great talk on your topic, packed with lots of valuable how-to tips they can use. The only mention of you and what you do should be in a brief introduction you give, typed out on a card to be read word for word, to the person from the group who will introduce you.

2. *Broaden your audience.* Want to bring your speech to a broader audience? Arrange to professionally record your presentation as an audio. Then duplicate the presentation on a CD or audiocassette with a nice label. Send an email or postcard to your mailing list telling them the title and contents of the talk, and offering the CD to them free.

I recently gave a talk on software marketing to a group of software publishers. I then mentioned the talk and offered a free tape recording in my monthly e-newsletter. Within twenty-four hours, I received more than two hundred requests for the tape, many from software companies interested in hiring me to write copy for them. From this one-paragraph mention in my e-newsletter, I landed an immediate twelve thousand dollars in copywriting business.

If you don't want to mail CDs or tapes, you can post your talk as a downloadable MP3 on your website and offer to send a link to it. Or, you can make a transcription, which you can send to prospects as a downloadable PDF file.

Part IX  Testing

CHAPTER 61

Tracking Responses

In direct mail, testing is the process of putting a letter or package in the mail, counting the replies, and coming to some conclusion based on the results. In traditional direct mail tests, two or more mailings or mailing factors are tested against one another simultaneously. For instance, you might test letter *A* against letter *B* to see which pulls more orders. Or, you might take letter *A* and mail it to two different lists, to see which list produces the better response. But testing doesn't have to be an *A* versus *B* proposition, even though that's the way it's traditionally viewed. Even if you only mail one package or one letter or use only one list at a time, you can still learn something from the mailing, as long as you keep track of the results.

Learning is the real purpose of direct mail testing. By counting replies and monitoring results, we learn what works for us in direct mail-and what doesn't. "Every time you do a mailing you should test something," writes James E. A. Lumley in his book, *Sell It by Mail*. "If you don't, you've wasted an opportunity to learn something about the prospects who respond to your offer." I agree with Lumley and urge you to measure leads and sales on every mailing you do.

Some say, "You can only test one thing versus another, such as package *A* versus package *B*." I disagree. If you mail five thousand letters and get two responses, you have learned something about how that particular audience of five thousand people responded to the particular product and offer you featured in that particular mailing.

Many industrial firms, for instance, can quickly and inexpensively discover whether a new product or service has appeal to a given market by doing a small test mailing. Using direct mail to test the waters in a new market can actually be much less expensive than hiring a market research firm or creating a new ad campaign.

Many direct mail experts also say, "There is no sense testing a mailing list unless it is large enough to allow for a full-scale mailing if the test mailing should be successful." In other words, don't test ten thousand names unless there are another ninety thousand people on the list you can mail to after you learn the test results. Again, I disagree. Even if your list is only ten thousand or even five thousand names, why not split it into two sections and test something—an offer, a product, a price? Why settle for just selling when you can also learn in the process?

To test, you must be able to track response. That is, when you receive a reply, you must be able to identify that reply as coming from a specific mailing or from a reader whose name was on a specific mailing list. There are several ways to do this. The simplest is to put a key number or code on the reply element. The code can be a series of numbers and letters in fine print tucked away in the corner of the reply card. Or, it can be worked into the address. For example, you might use the return address, "USA ENGINEERING ASSOCIATES, DEPT. DM-2, YORKTOWN, USA 54565" The code 'Dept. DM-2' tells us this reply card came from creative package two as opposed to package one.

The same thing can be done for telephone response, using either an extension ('call Ext. 123') or a person's name ('ask for Jennifer Smith'). If the person asks specifically for extension 123 or Jennifer Smith, the operator knows the call is in response to a specific mailing package.

This coding technique is also used in print ads. Try calling the toll-free numbers used in print ads; ask for the specific extension listed in the ad. Often, you are not switched and the operator who answers handles your call. This is because there is no such extension; the number is solely a tracking device.

If you are affixing labels to your reply card or order form, the mailing list owner can print a key code directly on the label. The charge for this service is nominal—usually about one dollar per thousand names. "Let your mailing house key the order cards or reply envelopes while labeling," advises Lee Epstein, CEO of a leading mailing services firm. "This will save you many on-press keying and inventory control headaches."

All the keying and coding in the world is useless if you don't train your people to keep track of response. Obviously it's very important to track all responses if you're going to have accurate test results. In particular, you must keep track of five types of responses:

1. People who respond by mailing or faxing the reply card or order form you have provided.

2. People who write on their own letterhead or send a company purchase order or a personal check without your order form.

3. People who phone in and ask for the person or extension you have specified.

4. People who call and do not specify the extension or person.

5. People who do not reply to you directly but are motivated by the mailing to contact their local sales representative or distributor.

Keeping track of responses two, four, and five above is, admittedly, a difficult task. You will always get some leads and sales for which you can't pinpoint the source. But be diligent about tracking those responses you can identify. The more accurate your counts, the more meaningful the conclusions you draw from your tests.

CHAPTER 62

Optimum Test Cell Sizing

How many test pieces of a direct mail package do you have to mail? Actually, test results are based on the number of responses—not the number of pieces mailed. So the real question is, "How many replies do we have to get back in order for the test to be considered statistically valid?" Different authorities quote different numbers. James Lumley says twenty responses. Ed Burnett, writing in *The Handbook of Circulation Management*, says between thirty and forty responses. Milt Pierce, who teaches the direct response copywriting workshop at New York University, says you need one hundred replies to get a statistically meaningful result. In my experience, the most accurate measure of how many replies you must receive (and therefore, of how many pieces you must mail) to get a statistically valid response is shown in a chart reprinted from *The Basics of Testing*, written by the late Ed McLean (**Figure 62-1**).

In this table, decline percentage tells you the maximum amount by which your rollout mailing (subsequent mailings to additional names on the same list following a successful test) will vary from the test. Let's say you select a twenty-five percent decline. That means, if you get a one percent response from the test, the rollout will generate no less than 0.75 percent response and no more than 1.25 percent response percent.

Figure 62-1. Percent of Decline

(The difference between the percent response generated in the test and the percent response you will get when rolling out to more names on the list after your test)		50%	25%	12.5%	6.25%
Here is your confidence level	75%	1.8	7.3	29.2	116.8
	85%	3.5	14.0	56.0	
	90%	6.6	26.2	104.8	
	95%	11.0	42.8		
	99%	21.7	86.9		

The degree of confidence tells you how sure you can be of staying within the decline percentage. If you choose an eighty-five percent level of confidence and a twenty-five percent decline percentage, you are saying, "I want there to be an eighty-five percent certainty that my rollout will stay within plus or minus twenty-five percent of the response rate my test generates."

We can determine how many pieces we need to test so that our test result gives us this level of confidence in our rollout. Take a look at the chart above. Go along the top line until you find twenty-five percent. Then go down the twenty-five percent column until you reach the eighty-five percent confidence level you want. The number of responses required to get this level of statistical validity from your test, as indicated in the box, is fourteen.

Therefore, if you anticipate a one percent response, then you need to mail 1,400 pieces per mailing list in your test (14 is 1 percent of 1,400). To be on the safe side, I'd make it an even two thousand. Therefore, when people ask me, "How many pieces do I need to mail to get a statistically valid test result?" my recommendation is two thousand names per list, based on the above analysis.

Is this accurate? The above formula was introduced to me not by Ed McLean (who was a good friend and valued colleague before he passed away) but by a large mailing list brokerage that has been involved in thousands of mailings. "We have been using this formula for more than thirty years, and we find, over and over, that you can get a statistically valid test result mailing two thousand names, not five thousand," says the president of the firm. I have since used it numerous times with clients doing smaller mailings, and have also found it to be valid.

CHAPTER 63

The Rollout Rule of Ten

Can the results of a small test mailing remain statistically valid regardless of how many additional names we mail? The answer is no. The rule of thumb for rollouts is that the total quantity you mail to should be no more than ten times the number of names you tested. Therefore, if you got a five percent response in a test of five thousand names, you can mail to as many as fifty thousand additional names on the list with the confidence that test results are repeatable in the rollout.

No matter how sorely you may be tempted, never do a rollout to more than ten times the test quantity. Results may not hold valid in these large numbers. Let's say you have a list of eighty thousand names. If you tested two thousand, you can rollout up to twenty thousand names and expect the decline percentage not to exceed the percentage you selected when using Ed McLean's table to conduct your test. Should results prove profitable on the twenty thousand names, you can then safely mail to the remainder of the list.

The booklet *444 Begged, Borrowed, Stolen & Even a Few Original Direct Response Marketing Ideas*, published by Rockingham/ Jutkins Marketing, 147 Richmond Street, El Segundo, CA 90245, presents a table showing you the probability that response from the rest of your mailing list will be similar to the test results (**Figure 63-1**).

Figure 63-1.

Size of test mailing	Response of test mailing	Anticipated response* (95% accurate)
2,000	1%	0.55 to 1.45%
2,000	2%	1.37 to 2.63%
2,000	3%	2.24 to 3.76%
2,000	4%	3.12 to 4.88%
2,000	5%	4.03 to 5.97%
2,000	10%	8.66 to 11.34%
2,000	20%	18.21 to 21.70%
10,000	1%	0.80 to 1.20%
10,000	2%	1.72 to 2.28%
10,000	3%	2.66 to 3.34%
10,000	4%	3.61 to 4.39%
10,000	5%	4.56 to 5.44%
10,000	10%	9.40 to 10.60%
10,000	20%	19.20 to 20.80%

*When mailing to remainder of mailing list.

How to read the table: Let's say you do a test mailing of two thousand pieces and get back one hundred replies for a five percent response. The chances are ninety-five out of one hundred that when you mail to the rest of the list, your response rate will be between 4.03 and 5.97 percent. Mailing to another two thousand prospects will therefore generate anywhere from eighty-one to one hundred-nineteen additional replies.

CHAPTER 64

What Should You Test?

What are the three most significant factors you can test? Number one is the mailing list. There may be half a dozen mailing lists that might be right for your offer, maybe more. You cannot assume you know which one is best, based on your personal prejudices. The only way to know for certain which list will pull best with your package is through a test mailing.

The second most important factor to test is the price. This applies mainly to mail-order selling. For instance, let's say you've published a one-thousand-page report on the telecommunications industry. How much will people pay for it? $195? $495? $1,200? You simply do not know until you test. And frequently, you will be amazed at how many people place orders at prices you thought were sky-high.

The third most important factor to test is the offer. For example, should you try for mail orders or leads? Should you offer a premium-a free gift? Will you get better response offering a gift item, such as a clock radio, or free information, such as a booklet or special report? You won't know which works best unless you test.

Make your mailing list broker your partner in testing. For instance, when you want to test a small portion of the list, ask your broker to supply you with what is called an nth name selection. How does this work? Let's say the list has seventy thousand names, and you are going to test-mail to seven thousand. In this example, seventy thousand divided by seven thousand equals an n of ten. That means the computer will select (for your test mailing) every tenth name as it randomly goes through the list. A random nth name selection ensures that you get an average, unbiased sample that represents a typical cross section of the list. This is much better than ordering the entire list and then picking the test names by hand. The danger of doing it that way is that you subconsciously select the names that will give you the best results (because you want your mailing to be a success). Test results are artificially elevated because of this favorable selection, and rollouts don't bring the results you would have expected.

Be selective. Don't test everything. Don't over test. Use tests only to ensure success or determine key information you really want or need to know. Below, in no particular order, are numerous factors that can be tested via direct mail.

products

premiums

formats

sizes

copy

colors

personalization

brochure versus no brochure

themes or sales appeals teasers

first-class versus third-class mail

business reply versus 'place stamp here'

toll-free numbers versus regular numbers

CHAPTER 65

Ten Essential Rules of Direct Mail Testing

There are perhaps hundreds or even thousands of rules for direct mail testing, but here are ten that I have found to be essential to obtain the best possible results from any direct mail program.

1. *Make every mailing a test.* To the extant possible, try to find a way to learn something about every mailing you send out. The process of improving the return on investment is one of learning and applying knowledge constantly.

2. *Establish goals for each test.* Determine the information you want to get out of the test, and the degree of reliability needed in your data, and then determine how much money you can afford to spend on the test.

3. *Test significant factors.* Design tests that test factors which make a substantial difference in direct mail results. These include the list, the offer, and—in mail order—the price.

4. *Test to find information you need to know.* There may be issues and information, specific to your industry, product or market, which have never been tested in direct mail before. If there is no reliable data from other sources, you have to be the pioneer in your field.

5. *Use direct mail to test ideas.* Design tests to settle questions, debates, and disagreements concerning strategy, format, lists, design, and copy. Instead of arguing theory, put ideas to the test.

6. *Test small.* Test even if you are using a small list with minimal or no rollout. Try to split the list for an *A* versus *B* test of a mailing package or a direct mail element, such as letter length or offer.

7. *Test consistently.* For example, if you are testing a single factor, such as an envelope teaser, all other factors in the two test packages must be identical-including the mailing list from which the names are taken and the date on which the packages are mailed. Control the variables and test oranges and oranges.

8. *Don't assume you know what will work.* Test to find out. More often than not, the results will shock you. Direct mail tests are great for shaking up so-called marketing and advertising 'experts' who think they know it all.

9. *Test anyway.* Even if you don't have enough money or names for a statistically valid test, test anyway. Some information is better than no information. Just be aware of the fact that the test is not statistically valid-and act upon the results accordingly.

10. *Learn more.* To learn more from a direct mail test, make a list of questions you want answered. Call up some of the people who did not respond, and ask them your questions. In addition to learning a great deal about why your mailing failed to moti-vate these people, you may be able to turn non-responders into responders and generate a lot of additional inquiries or orders.

Part X

Business Skills

CHAPTER 66

Increase Your Personal Productivity

The ability to work faster and get more done in less time isn't slavery; it's freedom. You're going to have the same big pile of stuff to do every day whether you want it or not. If you can be more efficient, you can get it done and still have some time left over for yourself, whether it's to read the paper, hike, jog, or play the piano. Here are ten ideas that can increase your personal productivity so you can get more done in less time.

1. *Master your PC.* Every engineer or manager who wants to be more productive should use a modern PC with the latest software. Doing so can double, triple, or even quadruple your output. Install on your PC the same software as your colleagues, other departments within your organization, vendors, and business partners use. The broader the range of your software, the more easily you can open and read files from other sources. Constantly upgrade your desktop to eliminate too-slow computer processes that waste your time, such as slow downloading of files or web pages. If you use the Internet a lot, get the fastest access you can. DSL is getting cheaper by the month and is well worth the money at its current price levels.

2. *Don't be a perfectionist.* "I'm a non-perfectionist," said Isaac Asimov, author of 475 books. "I don't look back in regret or worry at what I have written." Be a careful worker, but don't agonize

over your work beyond the point where the extra effort no longer produces a proportionately worthwhile improvement in your final product. Be excellent but not perfect. Customers do not have the time or budget for perfection; for most projects, getting ninety-five to ninety-eight percent of the way to perfection is good enough. That doesn't mean you deliberately make errors or give less than your best. It means you stop polishing and fiddling with the job when it looks good to you, and you don't agonize over the fact you're not spending another hundred hours on it. Create it, check it, and then let it go.

Understand the exponential curve of excellence. Quality improves with effort according to an exponential curve. That means early effort yields the biggest results; subsequent efforts yield smaller and smaller improvements, until eventually the miniscule return is not worth the effort. Productive people stop at the point where the investment in further effort on a task is no longer justified by the tiny incremental improvement it would produce. Aim for one hundred percent perfection, and you are unlikely to be productive or profitable. Consistently hit within the ninety to ninety-eight percent range, and you will maximize both customer satisfaction as well as return on your time investment. "Perfection does not exist," wrote Alfred De Musset. "To understand this is the triumph of human intelligence; to expect to possess it is the most dangerous kind of madness."

3. *Free yourself from the pressure to be an innovator.* As publisher Cameron Foote observes, "Clients are looking for good, not great." Do the best you can to meet the client's or your boss's requirements. They will be happy. Do not feel pressured to reinvent the wheel or create a masterpiece on every project you take on. Don't be held up by the false notion that you must uncover some great truth or present your boss with revolutionary ideas and concepts. Most successful business solutions are just common sense packaged to meet a specific need. Eliminate performance pressure.

Don't worry about whether what you are doing is different or better than what others have done before you. Just do the best you can. That will be enough.

4. *Switch back and forth between different tasks.* Even if you consider yourself a specialist, do projects outside your specialty. Inject variety into your project schedule. Arrange your daily schedule so you switch off from one assignment to another at least once or twice each day. Variety, as the saying goes, is indeed the spice of life.

Approximately seventy to ninety percent of what I am doing at any time is in familiar tasks within my area of expertise. This keeps me highly productive. The other ten to thirty percent is in new areas, markets, industries, or disciplines outside my area of expertise. This keeps me fresh and allows me to explore things that captivate my imagination but are not in my usual schedule of assignments.

5. *Don't waste time working on projects you don't have yet.* Get letters of agreement, contracts, purchase orders, and budget sign-offs before proceeding. Don't waste time starting the work for projects that may not come to fruition. An official approval or go-ahead from your boss or customer makes the project real and firm, so you can proceed at full speed, with the confidence and enthusiasm that come from knowing you have been given the green light.

6. *Make deadlines firm but adequate.* Of one hundred fifty executives surveyed by AccounTemps, thirty-seven percent rated the dependable meeting of deadlines as the most important quality of a team player (cited in *Continental* magazine, October 1997, page 44). Productive people set and meet deadlines. Without a deadline, the motivation to do a task is small to nonexistent. Tasks without assigned deadlines automatically go to the bottom of your priority list. After all, if you have two reports to file and one is due a week from Thursday and the other due "whenever you can get around to it," which do you suppose will get written first?

Often you will collaborate with your supervisor or customer in determining deadlines. Set deadlines for a specific date and time, not a time period. For example: "due June 23 by 3 pm or sooner," not "in about two weeks." Having a specific date and time for completion eliminates confusion and gives you motivation to get the work done on time. At the same time, don't make deadlines too tight. Try to build in a few extra days for the unexpected, such as a missing piece of information, a delay from a subcontractor, a last-minute change, or a crisis on another project.

7. *Protect and value your time.* Productive people guard their time more heavily than the gold in Fort Knox. They don't waste time. They get right to the point. They may come off as abrupt or dismissive to some people. But they realize they cannot give everyone who contacts them all the time each person wants. They choose who they spend time on and with. They make decisions. They say what needs to be said, do what needs to be done and then move on.

Assign a dollar value to your time. If you work forty hours a week, fifty weeks a year, that comes to two thousand hours a year. To calculate your hourly rate, divide your salary by two thousand. Example: $75,000 annual salary divided by two thousand hours comes to $37.50 an hour. Productive people can tell you in an instant the worth of their time, because they've already done this calculation and committed the answer to memory. Productive people weigh the effort required for a specific activity, and the return it will produce, against the cost of the time based on the dollar value of their hour. For instance, if my time is worth $37.50, and I spend an hour driving to a discount store to save ten dollars on supplies, I have not used my time wisely—I am $27.50 in the hole. On the other hand, if I saved one thousand dollars on a new computer for the same trip, it obviously was worth the time.

8. *Stay focused.* As Robert Ringer observed in his best-selling book, *Looking Out for Number One*, successful people apply themselves to the task at hand. They work until the work gets done.

They concentrate on one or two things at a time. They don't go in a hundred different directions. My experience is that people who are big talkers—constantly spouting ideas or proposing deals and ventures—are spread out in too many different directions to be effective. Efficient people have a vision and focus their activities to achieve that vision.

9. *Set a production goal.* Stephen King writes 1,500 words every day except his birthday, Christmas, and the Fourth of July. Steinway makes eight hundred pianos in its German plant every year. Workers and organizations that want to meet deadlines and be successful set a production goal and make it. Individuals who truly want to be productive set a production goal, meet it, and then keep going until they can do no more or run out of time for the day.

Joe Lansdale, author of *Bad Chili* and many other novels, says he never misses his productivity goal of writing three pages a day, five days a week. "I'm not in the mood, I don't feel like it—what kind of an excuse is that?" Lansdale said in an interview with *Publisher's Weekly* (September 29, 1997). "If I'm not in the mood, do I *not* go to the chicken plant if I've got a job in the chicken plant?"

10. *Do work you enjoy.* In advising people on choosing their life's work, David Ogilvy, founder of the advertising agency Ogilvy & Mather, quotes a Scottish proverb that says, "Be happy while you're living; for you're a long time dead." The Tao Te Ching says, "In work, do what you enjoy." When you enjoy your work, it really isn't work. To me, success is being able to make a good living while spending the workday in pleasurable tasks. You won't love every project equally, of course. But try to balance must-do mandatory tasks with things that are more fun for you. Seek assignments that are exciting, interesting, and fulfilling.

Can you train yourself to like work better and enjoy it more? Motivational experts say we do have the ability to change our attitudes and behavior. "Attitude is a trap or it is freedom. Create your own," writes Judy Crookes in *Inner Realm* magazine. "Enjoy your achievements as well as your plans," advised Max Ehrmann in his 1927 essay "Desiderata." "Keep interested in your own career, however humble; it is a real possession in the changing fortunes of time."

CHAPTER 67

Writing in the Internet Age

A while back I got an email from Matthew Budman, who is the Managing Editor of *Across the Board*, a magazine published by the Conference Board for senior-level executives at large corporations. Mr. Budman asked me to comment on an article on business writing two authors had submitted for publication in the magazine. The simple premise of the article was that, even in our technological era, writing skills are more important than ever. I'm not sure why he chose me as someone from whom he wanted commentary on business writing. It may be that I've written a couple of books on business writing including *The Elements of Business Writing* (Alyn & Bacon). But whatever the reason for my selection, the lead line of the *Across the Board* article (actually the subhead) caught my eye, and generated an immediate and visceral reaction from me. Here was the reply I gave him:

> Dear Mr. Budman:
>
> I'd like to believe your article subhead, 'In an age of technology, writing skills are more important than ever.' But I'm not convinced.
>
> My theory is that the Internet has and will continue to diminish the importance of writing skills and the quality of writing over time. The reason: pre-Internet, documents were printed, with considerable expense invested in the

design and reproduction. Therefore, publishers and other content producers would take pains to 'get it right.' After all, once the piece was printed, correcting a typo, grammatical error, or awkward sentence meant going back to press—again at considerable expense. In the Internet era, documents are increasingly electronic files posted on a website. Making corrections is easy, and in fact a whole new category of software—content management systems (CMS)—has evolved to manage these changes.

Now that content producers realize mistakes are quick, easy, and inexpensive to correct, they are not as concerned with getting it right the first time. As a result, they are not as particular about the quality of the writing, editing, and even thinking their organizations publish. So, it seems to me that, if anything, writing skills are less important in an age of technology, rather than more important.

Also, the Internet has sped up the pace of business and society. The primary attribute valued today in writing or any other product or service is speed, and it is an attribute to which quality often takes a back seat.

Does this mean that in direct marketing, copy is no longer king? No, because direct marketing is the one remaining communications method where good writing *is* more important than ever. With postage, printing, and other costs continually climbing, and response rates down across the board, it is more difficult than ever to get a strong control in the mail, one generating a good return on investment and likely to last one or two years, or longer. Worse, our prospects are bombarded by more communications than ever. There are literally millions of websites they can visit, and over eight hundred channels of television they can watch. Not to mention all the pop-up ads and spam they receive each day. With all that information competing for the prospect's attention, you have to work extra hard to make your mailing—whether print or online—stand out and grab the prospect's attention. And of course that means one thing primarily: strong copy. Though of course, graphics can help.

Lists and offers are tremendously important. But you can identify, fairly quickly and easily, those lists and offers that work best for your product. Once you've found the right lists and offers, then the only additional leverage you have for boosting response is through—you guessed it—copy. Ironically, while I believe the Internet may have diminished the importance of most kinds of writing, *our* type of writing—direct response copywriting—has *grown* in importance, not only offline but online as well. As Nick Usborne points out in his book *Net Words*, "Go to your favorite website, strip away the glamour of the design and technology, and you're left with words—your last, best way to differentiate yourself online."

The value society places on writing may be cyclical. When I was a youth in the 1960s, for instance, novels were an important art form as well as a vehicle for social change. Today we live in a different world. "We do live in a non-book age," says James Mustich Jr., owner of The Common Reader, a mail-order book catalog. "TV, the Internet, and other media now play a much greater role than books in determining the conversation of our culture, so much so that they threaten to overpower and drown out the more contemplative modes of experience, including book reading." Perhaps the pendulum will swing the other way again. But one thing is certain: any writing that can generate a return on investment for the publisher or marketer who buys the right words can command a premium price from the author. And whether you're online or offline, if you're selling something directly off the page or off the screen, those right words are your copy. So, in direct marketing, copy is still king.

CHAPTER 68

How to Get Out of a Slump

Getting out of a slump—whether in marketing, sales, or your career—is not difficult, though it often requires persistence. The problem is that most people either don't realize what they have to do to reverse a slump, or they are not willing to do it. I have developed a three-part strategy for overcoming a slump that works for both business and personal setbacks. The problem is that the formula is so simple. It contains a total of seven words. It is *so* simple that you may be tempted to dismiss it, even thought it has worked for me and hundreds of other individuals. Here is the formula for getting out of a slump:

1. Do something.
2. Do more.
3. Keep doing it.

Let's examine the three parts in more detail:

1. *Do something.* Do I mean do anything, no matter how random? Well, no. But almost. Most people in a slump spend most of their time worrying, ruminating, and planning. They suffer from *analysis paralysis.* They become so obsessed making their next step perfect, they never take it. You can only reverse a slump through action, so you've got to act—now! Not sure whether idea A makes sense? Do it anyway. Not sure whether to take path X or path Y?

Pick one and go forward. The very fact that you are taking action, instead of getting stuck in inaction, will automatically start you on the road to recovery.

2. *Do more.* There are two common reasons why people fail. One is that they don't do the work required to get the results they want. Putting into action just one or two ideas may help, but it's probably not enough to totally solve your problem. To get out of a slump requires that you take what motivational speaker Anthony Robbins calls *massive action.* How to implement this strategy: decide how much activity you think you really need to get fully out of your slump. Then do at least twice that amount.

3. *Keep doing it.* The second reason people fail is that they give up too early. Not everything you try will work. If you try one thing, then a second, then a third, and they all fail, do you give up? No. You try something else. Eventually one thing works OK. Another works better. And before you know it, you're well on the road to turning your situation around. But don't just forge ahead blindly. Evaluate the results of each effort. A corollary to step three is: do more of what's working, less of what's not working.

There you have it: three steps—seven words. Simple? Yes. Does it work? Absolutely. Try it and see for yourself.

Websites

www.awaionline.com
Home study courses and conferences on copywriting.

www.monthlycopywritinggenius.com
Monthly Copywriting Genius
Regular reviews of winning promotions and interviews with the copywriters who wrote them.

www.smallbusinessadvocate.com
The Small Business Advocate
Radio show and website dedicated to small business.

www.theadvertisingshow.com
The Advertising Show
Radio show on advertising.

www.agora-inc.com/reports/700SCBMO/W700D643/
Mailbox Millionaire
Home-study course on how to start and run a profitable direct response business.

Appendix II

E-Newsletters

Bencivenga's Bullets

www.bencivengabullets.com

Master copywriter Gary Bencivenga's can't-miss e-newsletter based on his decades of tested results.

Early to Rise

www.earlytorise.com

Daily e-newsletter on business success, wealth, and health by marketing guru Michael Masterson.

Excess Voice

www.nickusborne.com/excess_voice.htm

Nick Usborne's e-newsletter on online copywriting. Informative and great fun.

Marketing Minute

www.yudkin.com/markmin.htm

Weekly marketing tip from consultant Marcia Yudkin.

Paul Hartunian's Million-Dollar Publicity Strategies

www.prprofits.com

Great marketing e-newsletter focusing on publicity.

The Copywriter's Roundtable

www.jackforde.com

John Forde's superb e-newsletter on copywriting.

The Direct Response Letter

www.bly.com

My monthly e-newsletter on copywriting and direct marketing.

The Success Margin

Ted Nicholas's must-read marketing e-zine.

www.tednicholas.com

Appendix III
Periodicals

Advertising Age
711 Third Avenue
New York, NY 10017-4036
Tel: (212) 210-0100
http://www.adage.com
Contains in-depth coverage of newsworthy events in the advertising
business, with a strong focus on ad agencies.

Adweek
(Eastern Edition)
770 Broadway
New York, NY 10003
Tel: (646) 654-5421
Fax: (646) 654-5365
http://www.adweek.com
Offers readers a blend of advertising news, features, how-to articles,
and columns.

B-to-B
360 North Michigan Avenue
Chicago, IL 60601
http://www.btobonline.com
Covers advertising, sales, and marketing of products and services sold
to business and industry. It's a "must read" for industrial, high-tech,
medical, and financial copywriters.

Direct
http://www.directmag.com
Monthly tabloid covering the direct response industry.

Direct Marketing
224 Seventh St
Garden City, NY 11530
Tel: (516) 746-6700
http://www.dmcny.org
For readers involved in direct response marketing—direct mail, mail
order, telemarketing, Internet marketing. Published monthly.

DM News
Editorial and Advertising Office
100 Avenue of the Americas
New York, NY 10013
Tel: (212) 925-7300
Fax: (212) 925-8752
http://www.dmnews.com
A newspaper-style tabloid. Coverage is similar to Direct Marketing,
but articles are briefer and more oriented toward late breaking news
rather than general information. But DM News also publishes several
helpful how-to articles in each issue. Published weekly.

Public Relations Journal
33 Maiden Lane, 11th Fl.
New York, NY 10038-5150
Tel: (212) 460-1400
Fax: (212) 995-0757
http://www.prsa.org
This is the official monthly magazine of the Public Relations Society
of America, a society of public relations professionals. Copywriters
just getting into public relations can learn a lot from this magazine
on how to write material that editors will read and publish.

Sales and Marketing Management
770 Broadway 7th Floor
New York, NY 10003
Tel: (800) 641-2030
Fax: (646) 654-5355
http://www.salesandmarketing.com
A monthly magazine for sales managers and marketing managers.
Sales and Marketing Management runs informative articles on all
facets of marketing, including advertising. Most of the articles are
brief and instructive.

Target Marketing
1500 Spring Garden Street, Suite 1200
Philadelphia, PA 19130
Tel: (215) 238-5300
Fax: (215) 238-5270
www.targetonline.com
Monthly magazine covering direct marketing.

Appendix IV

Books

All Marketers Are Liars: The Power of Authentic Stories in a Low-Trust World by Seth Godin (Portfolio, 2005, hardcover, 186 pages, $23.95).
Experienced direct marketers know that, executed by a talented copywriter, a sales letter that tells an engaging story can become a breakthrough control. Godin's book spotlights the important of storytelling in marketing, and explains why a good story can often be a much more effective selling tool than a conventional features-and-benefits presentation.

Deadly Persuasion: Why Women and Girls Must Fight the Addictive Power of Advertising by Jean Kilbourne (The Free Press, 1999, hardcover, 366 pages).
An activist author, Kilbourne has written an anti-advertising book. But it's packed with examples and case studies of ad campaigns that have been especially successful throughout the years selling products to women.

Driven: How Human Nature Shapes Our Choices by Paul Lawrence and Nitin Nohria (Jossey-Bass, 2002, hardcover, 315 pages, $28).
Two Harvard professors claim that all human choices are controlled by four drives: to acquire, to bond, to learn, and to defend.

Influence: The Psychology of Persuasion, Revised Edition by Robert B. Cialdini (William Morrow, 1993. paperback, 320 pages, $15).
A fascinating compilation of numerous psychological experiments and observations designed to show how we are influenced and persuaded by the actions and words of others.

Libey and Pickering on RFM and Beyond by Donald R. Libey and Christopher Pickering (MeritDirect Press, 2005, hardcover, 338 pages, $59).
A classic, updated and expanded text on Recency, Frequency and Monetary Value as the cornerstone analytic of direct marketing for all channels. This book is a Masters Course of direct marketing and contains huge amounts of knowledge and wisdom on how to improve multi-channel customer and prospect profits using advanced RFM (and other strategies and tactics). A 'must-have' and 'must-read' for any direct marketing professional.

Same Game New Rules: 23 Timeless Principles for Selling and Negotiating by Bill Caskey (Winpointe Publishing, 2005, paperback, 207 pages).
Caskey has written one of the most sensible, practical books ever written on face-to-face selling, with twenty-three principles that can quickly make you a more effective salesperson.

Selling Dreams: How to Make Any Product Irresistible (Simon & Schuster, 1999, Gian Luigi Longinotti-Buitoni, hardcover, 333 pages, $26).
In this book, the president of Ferrari North America reveals his secrets for creating an intensive, red-hot desire in consumers to own your product

Who Am I? The 16 Basic Desires That Motivate Our Actions and Define Our Personalities by Steven Reiss (Berkley Books, 2005, paperback, 280 pages, $13.95).
Reiss argues that all human actions are driven by one or more of sixteen basic human desires. These include curiosity, idealism, eating, status, and the desire for acceptance.

Why We Buy: The Science of Shopping by Paco Underhill (Simon & Schuster, 1999, hardcover, 255 pages, $25).
This book explores how consumer purchase decisions are influenced and made in retail settings including stores, restaurants, and showrooms; in other words, how and why people shop.

Selling It: The Incredible Shrinking Package and Other Marvels of Modern Marketing by Leslie Ware (W.W. Norton & Company, 2002, paperback, 202 pages, $15.95).
Ware, a columnist for watchdog publication *Consumer Reports,* has written an expose of deceptive and fraudulent advertising, illustrated with dozens of examples. Some are blatant cheats, but many others are instructive and absolutely fascinating.

Sanders, Tim, *The Likeability Factor: How to Boost Your L-Factor and Achieve Your Life's Dreams* by Tim Sanders (Crown, 2005), hardcover, 224 pages, $23.
The premise of this book is that you succeed when people like you. The author applies this premise to advertising, and says the advertisements that consumers like best are also the ones that will do the best job of selling them on the product, a claim some seasoned direct marketers may argue.

The Irresistible Offer: How to Sell Your Product or Service in 3 Seconds or Less by Mark Joyner (John Wiley & Sons, 2005), hardcover, 219 pages, $21.95.
This is a first: the only full-length marketing book on offers, Reading it forces you to spend several hours thinking about nothing but offers, which is an invaluable exercise for every direct marketer.

How to Write a Good Advertisement by Vic Schwab (Wilshire Book Company, 1962).
A common-sense course in how to write advertising copy that gets people to buy your product or service, written by a plain-speaking veteran mail-order copywriter in 1960.

My First 50 Years in Advertising by Max Sackheim (Prentice-Hall, 1970).
Another plain-speaking, common-sense guide that stresses salesmanship over creativity, and results over awards. The author was one of the originators of the Book of the Month Club.

The Robert Collier Letter Book by Robert Collier (Robert Collier Publications, 1937).
How to write sales letters with numerous examples of classic mail-order letters.

Reality in Advertising by Rosser Reeves (Alfred A. Knopf, 1961).
The book in which Reeves introduced the now-famous concept of USP (the Unique Selling Proposition).

Breakthrough Advertising by Eugene Schwartz (Boardroom, 2004).
A copywriting guide by one of the greatest direct response copywriters of the 20th century.

Tested Advertising Methods, Fifth Edition by John Caples, revised by Fred Hahn (Prentice-Hall, 1997).
An updated edition of John Caples' classic book on the principles of persuasion as proven through *A/B* spit tests.

Confessions of an Advertising Man by David Ogilvy (Atheneum).
Charming autobiography of legendary ad man David Ogilvy, packed with useful advice on how to create effective advertising.

Scientific Advertising by Claude Hopkins (Bell Publishing, 1920).
A book on the philosophy that advertising's purpose is to sell, not entertain or win creative awards, and how to apply this philosophy to create winning ads.

Method Marketing by Denny Hatch (Bonus Books, 1999).
A book on how to write successful direct response copy by putting yourself in the customer's shoes. Packed with case histories of modern direct response success stories, including Bill Bonner of Agora Publishing, and Martin Edelston of Boardroom.

Advertising Secrets of the Written Word by Joseph Sugarman (DelStar, 1998).
How to write successful advertising copy by a modern master of the space ad.

Appendix V
Organizations

www.marketing.org
Business Marketing Association
Trade Association for business-to-business marketers

www.the-dma.org
Direct Marketing Association
Trade association for direct marketing

www.newsletters.org
Newsletter and Electronic Publisher's Association
Trade association for newsletter publishers

www.americanconsultantsleague.com
American Consultants League
Professional association for consultants

Appendix VI
Vendors

For referrals to mailing list brokers, graphic artists, website designers, and other vendors you need to help you implement marketing campaigns, go to:

http://www.bly.com/newsite/Pages/vendors.html

Appendix VII
Recommended Products

For more information on marketing books, e-books, courses, and programs Bob Bly recommends, visit these two sites:

www.blysentme.com

www.internetmarketinghallofame.com

About the Author

Bob Bly is an independent copywriter and consultant with more than twenty years of experience in business-to-business, high-tech, industrial, and direct marketing.

He has written copy for over one hundred clients, including Network Solutions, ITT Fluid Technology, Medical Economics, Intuit, Business & Legal Reports, and Brooklyn Union Gas. Awards include a Gold Echo from the Direct Marketing Association, an IMMY from the Information Industry Association, two Southstar Awards, an American Corporate Identity Award of Excellence, and the Standard of Excellence award from the Web Marketing Association.

Bob is the author of more than fifty books including *The Complete Idiot's Guide to Direct Marketing* (Alpha Books) and *The Copywriter's Handbook* (Henry Holt & Co.). His articles have appeared in numerous publications such as *DM News, Writer's Digest, Amtrak Express, Cosmopolitan, Inside Direct Mail,* and *Bits & Pieces for Salespeople.*

Bob Bly has presented marketing, sales, and writing seminars for such groups as the U.S. Army, Independent Laboratory Distributors Association, American Institute of Chemical Engineers, and the American Marketing Association. He also taught business-to-business copywriting and technical writing at New York University.

Bob writes sales letters, direct mail packages, ads, email marketing campaigns, brochures, articles, press releases, white papers, websites, newsletters, scripts, and other marketing materials clients need to sell their products and services to businesses. He also consults with clients on marketing strategy, mail order selling, and lead-generation programs.

Prior to becoming an independent copywriter and consultant, Bob was advertising manager for Koch Engineering, a manufacturer of process equipment. He has also worked as a marketing communications writer for Westinghouse Defense. Bob Bly holds a

B.S. in chemical engineering from the University of Rochester and has been trained as a Certified Novell Administrator (CNA). He is a member of the American Institute of Chemical Engineers and the Business Marketing Association.

He has appeared as a guest on dozens of television and radio shows including *The Advertising Show*, Bernard Meltzer, Bill Bresnan, CNBC, and CBS' *Hard Copy*. He has been featured in major media ranging from the *Los Angeles Times* and *Nation's Business* to the *New York Post* and the *National Enquirer*.

Bob Bly
22 E. Quackenbush Avenue
Dumont, NJ 07628
Tel: (201) 385-1220   Email: rwbly@bly.com
Fax: (201) 385-1138   URL: www.bly.com

ABOUT THIS BOOK

The text of this book is composed in 11-point ITC Galliard, a typeface designed by Matthew Carter in 1978 for the International Typeface Corporation and based on the work of the sixteenth-century letter cutter Robert Granjon.

The paper used is 60# Nature's Natural, a fifty percent post consumer recycled paper, processed chlorine free. The book's printer, Thomson-Shore, Inc., is a member of Green Press Initiative, a nonprofit program dedicated to supporting authors, publishers, and suppliers in their efforts to reduce their use of fiber obtained from endangered forests.

Jacket and text design by Angela Schmitt of West Des Moines, Iowa.

NOTES

NOTES

NOTES